Praise for This Book

"A must-read book for all the stock option tax issues that challenge even the IRS. This updated and greatly expanded second edition provides employees, executives, and advisors with highly readable wisdom to profit from their equity compensation." *Bruce Brumberg, Editor-in-Chief, myStockOptions.com*

"A very good overview of the tax and financial planning implications of stock options, written in a way that's useful to experts and understandable to those who are not."—*Corey Rosen, Executive Director, National Center for Employee Ownership*

"This book does a great job of explaining the rules so a participant can gain the most value from stock options while avoiding common mistakes and pitfalls."—*Gordon Rapkin, Executive Vice President, Chief Marketing Officer, Transcentive*

"A comprehensive information resource for employees, explaining as simply as possible the complexities of stock options."—*Debra Sherman, Foundation for Enterprise Development*

"Should be required reading for anybody receiving options as compensation."—*Roy Lewis, co-author, The Motley Fool's Investment Tax Guide*

> ▪ The Certified Equity Professional Institute has designated *Consider Your Options* as required reading for those seeking CEP Level I certification.

Praise for Our Web Site (fairmark.com)

Also by the Author

Capital Gains, Minimal Taxes: The Essential Guide for Investors and Traders

Consider Your Options

Get the Most from Your Equity Compensation

2004 Edition

Kaye A. Thomas

A Plain Language Guide From
FAIRMARK PRESS INC. LISLE, ILLINOIS

Consider Your Options
Get the Most from Your
Equity Compensation

This printing of *Consider Your Options: Get the Most from Your Equity Compensation* reflects relevant legal authorities as of October 31, 2003.

Published by:

Fairmark Press Inc.
P.O. Box 353
Lisle, Illinois 60532

Cover design by Abacus Graphics, Oceanside, California

Publisher's Cataloging-in-Publication Data
Thomas, Kaye A.
    Consider your options : get the most from your equity
compensation / Kaye A. Thomas. – 2004 ed.
    p. cm.
    Includes bibliographical references and index.
    LCCN: 99-91685
    ISBN: 0-9674981-3-9

    1. Employee stock options--Law and legislation--United States--Popular works. 2. Deferred compensation--Taxation--Law and legislation--United States--Popular works. I. Title.

KF6379.Z9T46 2000   343.7305'242
                              QBI99-1864

Table of Contents

About the Author

Kaye Thomas has over 20 years of experience dealing with tax matters relating to business transactions, finance and compensation. Much of that experience is in advising companies on how to establish and maintain equity compensation arrangements, and individuals on how to manage those benefits.

More recently he is founder of National Board of Certified Option Advisors Inc. (on the web at **www.nbcoa.com**), an organization formed to help tax professionals and other financial advisors develop and demonstrate expertise in dealing with employee stock options and other forms of equity compensation, and to help individual option holders identify professionals who have such expertise.

Kaye also maintains a free web site called the *Tax Guide for Investors* at **www.fairmark.com**, providing hundreds of pages of plain language tax guidance. The web site also features a message board where Kaye and other tax professionals respond to questions and comments from readers.

Kaye's law degree is from Harvard Law School, where he served as an editor of the *Harvard Law Review* and graduated *cum laude* in 1980.

Acknowledgments

People who took time to review parts of an earlier version of this book and offer helpful comments include Rich Carreiro, Sean Coffey, David desJardins, Bob Franzen, CPA, John Goldsbury, Lewis Metzger, Frank Russo, Greg Stathis, Carol Tomkovich and Priscilla Walther. Thanks to their generosity the book is more complete, accurate and understandable.

Special thanks go to Barbara Baksa, who drew on her experience as Senior Manager of Industry Education in the Business Solutions Group of E*TRADE Financial to suggest ways to make the book more useful, and to Curt Freeman, who seems to have the knowledge and insight to shed light on even the most obscure corner of the tax law.

Beth Mowry Thomas provides help and encouragement and, when needed, firm but gentle criticism.

None of these people had an opportunity to prevent my evil twin from inserting errors during final editing.

Part I
Laying the Foundation

Part I of this book provides the information you need to get the most out of all the other parts. Chapter 1 explains what's the big deal about *equity compensation*—stock and options—and why it's so important to handle them properly. Chapter 2 provides a bird's-eye view of the entire subject to give you a feel for what's coming.

There are certain things about stock, options and taxes that are almost never explained because "every idiot" knows them. Unfortunately, there are many normal, intelligent, educated adults who *don't* know these things—because hardly anyone ever bothers to explain them. The remaining chapters in Part I lay out the basics in plain language.

Part I Laying the Foundation

Chapter 1
The Buzz—and the Buzz Saw

The first edition of this book, published early in the year 2000, began with a cheery story about a secretary who retired as a millionaire after exercising stock options. Options were making many people wealthy in those days. That was the buzz—and taxes were the buzz saw that cut into those profits, especially for people who mishandled their options.

The stock market peaked shortly after the book came out, and many option holders ran into a different buzz saw. The collapse began with Internet companies that achieved stratospheric valuations without demonstrating the ability to achieve profits, then spread to overextended telecom companies and eventually decimated the prices of many technology firms. In this downturn, even terrific companies like Intel and Cisco Systems were not immune, losing 80% of their value before the dust cleared.

"Optionaires" were among those who suffered most. Many saw the value of their stock options plummet. Some made catastrophic mistakes that left them with tax debts far exceeding the value of their stock. Yet there were also those who managed to convert option wealth to other investments less susceptible to SDS: sudden disappearance syndrome.

In a sense, that's what this book is all about: getting from here to there. You're "here" when you hold stock options, an asset that can grow rapidly in value but can just as quickly dwindle. You're "there" when you've made the transition to a more permanent investment, typically a diversified portfolio of stocks and bonds. The goal of this book is to help you capture as much value as possible, net of taxes, without undue exposure to risk.

Feedback from readers of the first edition indicated they needed more guidance on planning. In particular, while the first edition was strong on taxes it was weak on investment-related issues. It was up to the reader to figure out when to exercise a stock option and whether to hold the stock after exercising. Those questions are complicated enough to trip up financial planning professionals, so it isn't surprising when option holders without training in this area falter. This edition includes ten new chapters on stock option planning. Some deal with general principles and others address specific strategies. While avoiding as much as possible the technical jargon of modern portfolio theory, the material on planning uses some of its main ideas. If there is one central theme, it is avoiding *uncompensated risk*—risk that doesn't contribute to the achievement of higher investment returns.

Understanding the value of an option is an aid in evaluating risk and return. The new material includes a discussion of the *Black-Scholes formula*, and offers something you won't find anywhere else: instructions on setting up a simple spreadsheet to calculate option values. In most cases you won't need this calculation to develop a strategy, but it's available if you find it useful.

Why Options Work

Stock options may have lost some of their luster in the sour stock market of the last two years, but options continue to be an excellent way to build wealth. They work for a simple reason: companies grow. That makes their stock and options go up in value. Whether you work for a startup that's looking to go public or an established industrial giant, growth—specifically, growth in earnings—is the goal. If you hold stock or options, your company's growth will add to your wealth.

The Unkindest Cut

Investors encounter various types of expenses that reduce their profits. Brokerage commissions, periodicals—even the cost of this book—cut into the amount of wealth you're accumulating. One expense is greater than all the rest: *taxes.*

The good news is that you have a fair amount of control over this expense. You can't change the rules or lower the rates, of course. Yet careful planning can reduce the pain. Generally, *you* determine when to exercise options and when to sell stock. You may have other planning opportunities as well, such as the *Section 83b election.* If you make the right moves, Uncle Sam gets a smaller piece of the pie.

Sadly, many holders of stock and options fail to seize these opportunities. They wake up to the fact that they have options when they're about to expire. Exercising the options becomes a fire drill, with no opportunity for planning. Much of the stock has to be sold right away to pay taxes. The beneficiary of this inattention is the United States Treasury.

If you find yourself in this situation, there's still plenty of help in this book, as it explains all the tax rules that apply when you exercise options and sell the stock. There's still more help here, though, for those who are willing to spend a little time planning their moves. Painful as it may be to study tax rules, the payoff can be handsome indeed.

Good Help Is Hard to Find

As equity compensation gains in popularity, more and more people are affected by these complicated tax rules. Yet the guidance on these rules is skimpy. The IRS puts out scores of information publications explaining all sorts of tax rules in great detail, yet devotes less than two pages in one publication to the tax rules for compensatory options. Alternative minimum tax? The IRS used to have a publication explaining AMT, but discontinued it several years ago.

A qualified tax professional may be able to guide you through the maze. Bear in mind, though, that some return preparers get most of their tax information from IRS publications, and we've already seen how little help they'll get from that source. Even the pros who use more sophisticated research materials may not run into these rules often enough to know all the ins and outs.

There's another problem in seeking professional advice on handling stock options. You often need a combination of tax expertise and investment expertise. Tax professionals tend to be cautious—and rightly so—when it comes to offering investment advice. At the same time, you can't expect your investment advisor to master all the arcane tax rules. It's important for *you* to be an informed member of the team that plans your option strategy.

www.fairmark.com

Some of the material in this book is drawn from the Fairmark Press *Tax Guide for Investors*, a free web site located at www.fairmark.com. While this book contains material that doesn't appear on the web site, it's also true that some topics touched on briefly here, such as the wash sale rule, receive a more thorough treatment on the web site. You're invited to visit that site for details on related tax issues. Significant developments relating to the topics in this book will be posted there as well. You'll also find a message board at fairmark.com where you can post questions on this subject, or comments about this book.

Chapter 2
The Big Picture

Compensation in stock and options can provide huge advantages for both the company and the workers who receive the compensation. It's fair to say that many companies couldn't survive in today's market without providing this form of compensation. What makes equity compensation better than cash?

Major advantages. Equity compensation helps the company in several ways. Compensation provided in this form doesn't absorb cash that may be needed for other corporate purposes. The company may be able to claim a deduction for the compensation, reducing its taxes and preserving even more cash. In some cases, the company may be able to provide this compensation without taking a "hit" to earnings for accounting purposes. By showing higher earnings the company makes investors happy and increases the market value of its stock.

The most important advantage of equity compensation, though, is its ability to attract, retain and motivate workers who can make the company prosper. Nothing is more important to a company's success than a motivated workforce. Compensation in stock and options gives the workers a real stake in the success of the company, and that's good for both the company and the workers.

Taxes. When it comes to taxes, equity compensation provides both advantages and disadvantages relative to cash. In some situations, it's possible for workers to obtain valuable rights, even amass significant wealth, without having to report income until the rights are cashed in. With cash, it's pay as you go. The flip side is that in some circumstances you *do* have to pay tax on your equity compensation, even before you've reduced your holdings to cash—perhaps even before it's *possible* to reduce your holdings to cash. In this situation you need to come up with money somewhere else to pay taxes on what you received. When this happens, careful planning is a necessity.

Shareholders. It may be useful to have in mind the perspective of other shareholders on compensation in stock and options. When a company issues shares as compensation, it increases the total number of shares outstanding. If the value of the company doesn't increase by a corresponding amount, the value per share is diluted. For this reason, shareholders—especially large, institutional shareholders—may be skeptical about some arrangements for equity compensation. Shareholders are the ultimate bosses of the corporation and generally have the right to approve equity compensation arrangements. If your company is less generous than you would like, it may be at least partly because existing shareholders want to protect their own equity.

Shareholders know, however, that what's good for the company will ultimately be good for them. The advantages mentioned above provide a convincing argument for equity compensation arrangements in general. A well-designed program will provide value for *everyone*, including the company's shareholders.

Property as Compensation

You're used to thinking of compensation as cash you receive for your services. Other types of income, such as interest and dividends, typically come in the form of cash, too. It may seem strange at first to report compensation income when you haven't received any cash.

That's exactly what the law requires you to do. The general rule is that whenever you receive stock or other property as compensation for services, you have to report the receipt of compensation income. You may have to report income and come up with money to pay the tax, even though you didn't receive any cash and can't sell the property! In some situations, though, you won't report income until a future event occurs.

If you're an employee, you may have *withholding* on your equity compensation. Of course the company won't withhold shares of stock and send them to the IRS. Somehow or other the withholding obligation has to be satisfied in cash. If you're not an employee (for example, a non-employee director or consultant), the withholding rules don't apply.

The amount of compensation you have to report depends on the *fair market value* of the property you receive. For publicly traded stock, fair market value is determined by the trading price. If your company isn't publicly traded, it may be more difficult to determine fair market value.

Stock Grants and Purchases

Companies sometimes provide equity compensation by making a *stock grant.* They simply give you the stock in return for your services. This is the simplest form of equity compensation, and the result is that you report equity compensation equal to the fair market value of the stock.

This assumes there are no strings attached to the stock grant—in other words, the stock is *vested.* Your company may say that you have to give the stock back if you quit working there within a specified period of time. In that case you don't report income until the end of that time period unless you file a *section 83b election* with the IRS (see Chapter 33). The reason you might do this is to avoid reporting *more* compensation income. If you delay reporting until the stock vests, you have to report compensation income equal to the fair market value of the stock *at that time*, which may be a lot higher than the value when you received it.

These rules apply also when you buy stock from the company. If you buy at a bargain price, you have to report compensation income equal to the difference between fair market value and the amount you paid. Even if you pay full fair market value, you may have to file a section 83b election if you've agreed to sell the stock back to the company under some circumstances.

Nonqualified Options

A *nonqualified option* is an option to buy the company's stock, other than an *incentive stock option* (described below). Companies can grant nonqualified options to employees and other service providers, such as non-employee directors and consultants. The rules for nonqualified options build on the rules for stock grants and purchases.

You don't report any income at the time you receive a nonqualified option. This is true even though the option may be a valuable property right that would result in gift tax if you gave it away. Instead, you generally report income at the time you exercise the option. At that time, you apply all the rules described above for purchases of stock in connection with services. You report compensation income equal to the difference between the fair market value of the stock and the amount you paid. If the stock isn't vested at the time you exercise the option, you won't report income until the stock vests unless you file a section 83b election.

Incentive Stock Options

An *incentive stock option* (ISO) is an option that meets various technical requirements set forth in the Internal Revenue Code. You must be an *employee* to receive an ISO. Non-employee directors and consultants aren't eligible.

The rules for incentive stock options build on the rules for stock grants *and* the rules for nonqualified options. You don't report income when you receive the options *or* when you exercise them and receive the stock. Instead, you report income when you *sell* the stock. Better still, if you hold the stock long enough, you'll be able to report long-term capital gain instead of compensation income. That makes this form of equity compensation very attractive to employees. But there are important qualifications.

One is the special holding period for capital gain treatment. You have to hold the stock until the *later* of two years after you received the option or one year after you exercised it. Otherwise you'll be treated (approximately) the same as if you received and exercised a nonqualified option.

More importantly, although you don't report income when you exercise the option, you report an adjustment under the *alternative minimum tax* (AMT). The adjustment is the same as the amount of compensation income you would report if you had a nonqualified option: the difference between fair market value and the price you paid for the stock. You could pay tax of 28% or more on this amount in the year you exercise your option. Under some complicated rules, you may recover some or all of this payment in the year you sell the stock. Planning for the AMT can be an intricate and painful process.

Employee Stock Purchase Plans

Some employers have broad-based plans permitting employees to purchase stock, often at a discount of 15% from the current value. If you participate in one of these plans, you won't report income until you sell the stock. At that time, you may have to report a portion of the sale price as compensation income rather than capital gain.

Chapter 3
Stock 101

What is stock? For some people, equity compensation is the first experience with owning stock. Even if you've previously owned or traded stock, you may not have a clear idea what you owned. This chapter explains what stock is, and also tells how to buy and sell stock.

What Is a Corporation?

Begin by thinking about what a *corporation* is. Any answer to that question is necessarily abstract, because a corporation isn't something you can see or touch. It doesn't physically exist. That's why people sometimes say a corporation is a *legal fiction*. That doesn't mean corporations aren't real. It just means their reality is . . . intangible.

The abstraction we call a corporation is a way of organizing the legal rights of people connected with a business enterprise. Here's a brief summary of the chief characteristics:

- Day-to-day management of the corporation is vested in the *officers*, and other people who work under the direction of the officers.

- The *board of directors* makes major policy decisions (often including adoption and administration of equity compensation arrangements), and has authority to appoint and remove officers.

- *Shareholders* vote on major decisions (often including approval of equity compensation arrangements adopted by the board of directors) and elect the directors.

Owning Stock

When you acquire stock, you're becoming a shareholder—the ultimate boss of the corporation. But you didn't work so hard for those shares just so you could vote for the directors. Shares of stock also represent economic ownership. The shareholders own the company. That's why stock has value.

Even at this level, though, things are pretty abstract. As a shareholder you have two economic rights: (1) the right to receive dividends, when and if the directors declare them, and (2) the right to receive a share of the liquidation proceeds if the company goes out of business. Yet many stocks are quite valuable even though they pay no dividends and the company's unlikely to liquidate at any time in the foreseeable future. That's OK: if the company has *assets*, and more importantly, a steady and rising stream of *earnings*, the market will recognize the value of the company in the price of its stock.

You should be aware that the price of a company's stock can plummet, sometimes for reasons outside the company's control. Every year, many corporations fail, leaving their shareholders with worthless stock. In the aggregate, though, stocks provide such a good investment that you almost *have* to own some if you want to be a successful investor, as explained in Chapter 38.

Stock Certificates

You may have seen, or even personally own, stock certificates. These are pieces of paper that document your ownership of one or more shares. Most often, when people buy and sell stocks through a broker, they never see the certificates. They simply get a statement from the broker saying that they own a certain number of shares. You don't need to have a certificate to be a shareholder. You may receive certificates in connection with your equity compensation, but it's also possible you'll own shares without ever receiving certificates.

Buying and Selling Shares

When you buy shares under a plan offered by your company, you have to follow the procedures set forth in the plan or in your option agreement. Many plans also provide a way for you to sell shares, too. It's possible, though, that you'll find yourself with stock certificates and not know how to sell them.

In this case, you need to establish an account with a stock broker. This may seem like an unfamiliar and even somewhat scary thing to do. In reality, nothing could be simpler. Brokers *love* to have people open new accounts, so they'll make it very easy for you to do so. It's pretty much like opening a bank account. You fill out some forms, including one that gives your social security number. You also give them some money—or some stock. They'll tell you the rest, including how you give an order to buy or sell stock.

If the only thing you need to do is sell the shares and get your hands on the money, you may as well go to a discount broker with a convenient office. Give more thought to your choice if you plan to continue using the brokerage account. Consider whether you need the kind of guidance and hand-holding you get from a full-service broker (where fees are higher), or whether you want to be able to use your computer to buy and sell stocks over the Internet. There are many brokers to choose from, and no single one is right for everyone.

Chapter 4
Income Tax 101

Many people pay income tax without understanding much about it. I often run into people, for example, who know that *deductions* are good, and *credits* are good, but don't have a clear idea of the difference between the two. To think intelligently about your equity compensation you need to understand the basic structure of the income tax—and also understand what your *tax bracket* is. Fortunately, these basics are quite simple.

Four Steps

Figuring your income tax involves four steps:

1. Find your *total income.*

2. Subtract your deductions: the result is your *taxable income.*

3. Apply the tax rates to find your tax.

4. Subtract your withholding and other payments and credits: the result is the tax you owe, or the refund you have coming.

Step 1: Total Income

The first step is to add up your *total income.* Total income includes many kinds of receipts: wages, interest, dividends, business and partnership income, amounts you receive from IRAs and pension plans, alimony, lottery winnings—and the list goes on. Of special interest: it includes your profit from sales of assets such as stock or real property—in other words, *capital gain.* But some items aren't included. For example, total income doesn't include inheritances or gifts you receive, or life insurance proceeds.

Step 2: Deductions

The second step in determining your income tax is to subtract the *deductions*. Deductions come in four main flavors:

Business deductions. These deductions are claimed as part of the calculation of business income, so they're actually part of the determination of total income in Step 1. But take note: deductions related to investment activities are *not* considered business deductions.

Adjustments. *Adjustments* are a special class of deductions you're allowed to claim even if you don't claim *itemized deductions* (see below). You claim your adjustments at the bottom of page 1 of Form 1040. Among the items here are your contributions to an IRA or other retirement plan, student loan interest, and alimony you paid. When you subtract your adjustments from total income, you arrive at an important number called *adjusted gross income.* On Form 1040, that's the last number on page 1 and also the number at the top of page 2.

Itemized deductions; standard deduction. Each year you're allowed to claim *itemized deductions* or the *standard deduction,* whichever is larger. Itemized deductions include such items as medical expenses, state and local taxes, mortgage interest and investment expenses. If those items don't add up to a large enough total, you claim the standard deduction instead. Your standard deduction depends on your filing status and is adjusted each year for inflation. Most people find that the standard deduction is larger than the total of their itemized deductions—at least, before they become homeowners. As your income grows, you're likely to see your itemized deductions grow also. When they become large enough, you should claim itemized deductions instead of the standard deduction.

> • For a single filer in 2004 (not blind or over age 65) the standard deduction is $4,850.

Exemptions. You're allowed a deduction just for being you: a personal exemption. You're also allowed an exemption for each person who qualifies as your *dependent*. Like the standard deduction, the exemption deduction is adjusted each year for inflation.

> • The personal exemption amount for 2004 is $3,100.

Taxable income. When you've subtracted all of these deductions from your total income, the result is your *taxable income*.

Step 3: Apply the Tax Rates

Once you know your taxable income, you apply the tax rates to find out your tax. Most people do this quite simply by looking up their taxable income in a table supplied with their tax form. If your income includes long-term capital gain, you have to perform a special calculation to obtain the benefit of the lower rate that applies to this type of income.

Step 4: Subtract Payments and Credits

The tax law allows you to claim certain *credits* that reduce the amount of tax you owe. For example, if you pay for child care, a portion of that expense may be allowed as a credit. And of course, you get credit for any tax you've already paid—including income tax your employer withheld from your paycheck and any estimated tax payments you made during the year. Subtract your credits and payments from your tax to find out how much you owe. If your payments exceed the tax, you're in luck: you have a refund coming!

Note that deductions and credits have very different effects on your tax. A deduction reduces your taxable income, before you apply the tax rates. That means a $100 deduction doesn't reduce your taxes by $100. If you're in the 25 percent tax bracket, a $100 deduction reduces your taxes by $25. A credit, on the other hand, reduces your tax directly. A $100 credit reduces your tax by $100.

Your Tax Bracket

Apart from knowing the basic structure of the income tax, there's one other basic concept you need to understand: your *tax bracket*. Knowing your tax bracket can help with your tax planning, because it tells you approximately how much value you'll get from a deduction, and also how much added tax you'll pay if you have additional income. Nearly everyone has heard of tax brackets and has a vague understanding of what they are, but there are widespread misconceptions about the precise concept.

Remember that Step 3 above involves applying the tax rates to your taxable income. Here's what really goes on. There are a series of tax rates, with the lowest being 10%. When you apply the tax rates, you're applying the lowest rate to your first chunk of taxable income, the next higher rate to the next chunk of taxable income, and so on. For example, a single filer in 2004 with taxable income of $50,000 will pay tax at the rate of 10% on the first $7,150 of taxable income, 15% on the next $21,900, and 25% on the rest. This isn't enough taxable income to reach the next tax rate, which is 28%.

Notice that in this example different parts of the income are taxed at different rates. That means the overall rate is a blend of these rates. But this person's *tax bracket* is 25%. Adding $1,000 to her income will increase her tax by $250; similarly, a $1,000 deduction will *decrease* her tax by $250.

Misconceptions. One of the misconceptions about tax brackets is that you may suffer some whopping hit of additional tax when you move into the next higher bracket. That doesn't happen. If your income is right at the top of the 25% bracket and you earn another $100 of income, you move into the 28% bracket. But all that means is you pay $28 of tax on that $100 of added income. You still pay the lower rates on your earlier income.

Another misconception is that your tax bracket somehow attaches to your normal amount of earnings, so that other types of income don't affect it. For example, suppose your normal earnings put you in the 25% bracket. Then you have some extraordinary added amount of income—perhaps you converted a traditional IRA to a Roth IRA, or had a large short-term capital gain. If your added income is large enough to cause you to pay tax at a higher rate, then it moves you into that higher bracket, at least for that year.

> ▪ Long-term capital gains won't move your other income into a higher bracket. In tax lingo, we say these gains, which are taxed at special, favorable rates, are "stacked on top of" ordinary income.

There's yet another misconception about tax brackets. Some people try to relate their tax bracket to the amount of tax withheld from their paychecks. But the withholding rate doesn't correspond to your tax bracket. Recall the example above where the overall rate was a blend of the rates that apply to different portions of taxable income. Withholding rates are designed to hit your blended rate, not your tax bracket. The actual amount withheld depends on your income level, the number of allowances you claimed, and certain other factors. If you're in the 25% bracket, adding $1,000 to your earnings will add $250 to your tax, but the amount added to your withholding may be somewhat larger or smaller.

Determining your tax bracket. Even if you prepare your own income tax return, you may not know what your tax bracket is because most people determine their tax by looking it up in a table that says, for example, if your taxable income is between $40,000 and $40,050, your tax is $6,744 (single filer, 2004). The blended rate is about 17%. But that doesn't tell you your tax bracket.

There are two ways to find your tax bracket. One is to look at that same table and see how much higher your tax would be if your income increased by $100. But there's a better way, and that is to look at the *tax rate schedules* that come in the instructions to Form 1040. Find the amount of *taxable income* on your tax return (income after all deductions) and see where it fits in the tax rate schedule for your filing status. Looking at the tax rate schedule is helpful because it tells you how close you are to moving into the next tax bracket. For example, if your taxable income places you in the 28% bracket, but just a few hundred dollars short of the 33% bracket, you know that a $20,000 bonus will be taxed mostly at 33%, even though your tax bracket before you receive the bonus is 28%.

Marginal rate. People sometimes refer to *marginal rate* as a synonym for tax bracket. Others use this term for a more precise concept. If you're in the 28% tax bracket, an added $100 of income won't necessarily result in $28 of extra tax. The added income may cause you to lose out on some deduction or credit you would otherwise claim, so the real tax cost of that $100 may be greater than $28. In situations where precision is important, you need to know your exact marginal rate, not your tax bracket. But you can only learn that through examining (or recalculating) your entire income tax return.

Chapter 5
Capital Gains 101

Most forms of equity compensation present the possibility that you will have *capital gains*. Even if you've never had capital gains before, you probably have at least a vague sense that they get special tax treatment, with a favorable tax rate. It's helpful to understand how the rules for capital gains and losses can help you—or hurt you.

Two Basic Flavors

All of the income and deductions you may have are divided into two categories: *ordinary* income and loss, and *capital* gain and loss. Ordinary income includes your wages, of course, and also includes many other types of income: interest, dividends, pension and IRA income, alimony income—the list goes on, because it includes everything *other than* capital gain.

So what is capital gain? Generally speaking, you have capital gain or loss when you sell a *capital asset*, which is basically anything of lasting value, other than something you sell as inventory to customers.

We'll see that equity compensation can result in ordinary income, capital gain, or some of both. In some cases, the amount of income you have from ordinary income rather than capital gain depends on when you exercise an option, or how long you hold your stock, or even whether you make a special filing with the IRS called a *section 83b election*.

Tax Treatment of Capital Gains

The most significant difference between capital gain and ordinary income is the tax rate for *long-term* capital gain.

This is capital gain from an asset you held more than a year: at least a year and a day. If you have a long-term capital gain that isn't wiped out by a capital loss, you pay tax on that gain at the rate of 15% (or 5%, to the extent the gain falls in what would be the 10% or 15% bracket for ordinary income).

That's a huge difference. Most people who have capital gains would otherwise pay tax at rates between 25% and 35%. Compared to those numbers, a 15% rate is *sweet*. And if you're in the 15% bracket, the ability to pay only 5% on your long-term capital gain is like getting a two-thirds off "sale price" on your taxes.

You may also have *short-term* capital gains. These are gains from sale of an asset you held one year or less. Notice that if you sell stock on the anniversary of the date you acquired it, your gain or loss is short-term. You need to hold one more day to get long-term gain or loss.

Short-term capital gain is taxed at the same rates as ordinary income. No special tax break there. But short-term capital gain can still be better than ordinary income. That's because of the way the tax law treats capital *losses*.

Tax Treatment of Capital Losses

Special rules apply to capital losses. Just like capital gains, you have to divide them between long-term and short-term. Then you apply them in the following order:

- First, deduct the loss against capital gains in the same category (long-term loss against long-term gain, short-term loss against short-term gain).

- Next, if you have overall loss in one category, deduct the loss against any gain that's left in the other category (long-term loss against short-term gain, or short-term loss against long-term gain).

- If you still have some capital loss left after these two steps, apply the loss against your ordinary income—but only up to $3,000 of capital loss.

- Any remaining amount of capital loss *carries over* to the next year, when you can use it just as if it was a brand-new loss for that year. If you still don't use all of it, you carry it to the next year, and so on.

Generally speaking, an *ordinary* deduction or loss is better than a capital loss. If you have an ordinary loss of $5,000, you don't have to worry about a $3,000 limit, and the loss will reduce your ordinary income. A *capital* loss will reduce your capital gain—the part of your income that may be taxed at a lower rate. Worse, if your capital loss is large enough, you may have to carry part of it to the next year, rather than using all of it to save taxes right away.

Basis

You don't know capital gains until you understand *basis*. Some people have a hard time with this concept, so don't worry if it doesn't seem obvious to you. The basic idea is that basis represents your investment in a particular asset.

For a simple example, suppose you buy 100 shares of stock through a broker. The stock is trading at $25, so you pay $2,500. On top of that you pay a $30 commission to the broker. Your *basis* for the stock is $2,530, ($25.30 per share) because that's what it cost to buy it.

There are many rules for determining basis in different situations, but most of them follow a fairly simple logic. For example, suppose the stock you bought in the previous example split two for one. Now you have 200 shares where you had 100 before. You didn't pay any additional money to acquire these shares, so your investment didn't increase. Your total basis stays the same, at $2,530, and your basis per share is now $12.65.

Basis includes reported income. There's one rule of particular importance when it comes to equity compensation. Generally, if you have to report income when you receive property, your basis includes the amount of income you reported. For example, if your employer grants stock to you worth $5,000, you'll report $5,000 of income—and you'll own the stock with a basis of $5,000. If you sell it for $5,600, you'll report a gain of $600, even though you never actually paid for the stock. It's as if your employer paid you $5,000 in cash and you used the money to buy the stock.

Amount realized. When you sell stock or other capital assets, you report gain or loss based on the difference between the *amount realized* and your basis. The amount realized is what you received for the sale, including any debts that attached to the property. If you sell stock through a broker, the amount realized is the selling price of the stock minus the brokerage commission and any other expenses of sale.

Form 1099-B. When you sell stock through a broker, you'll receive a form that indicates the amount realized. Some people panic when they see *Form 1099-B* because it reports the entire amount realized, not just the *gain.* You may hold stock with a basis of $7,000 and sell it for $9,000 for a $2,000 gain. The form you get from the broker simply says you sold for $9,000. It's up to you to determine your basis and correctly report the gain or loss on your tax return.

Capital Gain Planning

Planning for capital gains can run into complexities that test the patience of even the most capable tax advisor. Yet anyone who holds capital assets can be aware of basic capital gain planning techniques. Tax planning shouldn't dictate your handling of capital assets in all cases, but you should take these points into account in making your decisions.

Avoid short-term gains. Short-term capital gains are taxed at the same rates as ordinary income, while long-term capital gains receive favorable treatment. Generally speaking, you have it within your power to convert short-term capital gains into long-term capital gains, through the simple expedient of postponing sales. If you're selling at a gain, try to avoid selling shares you've held a year or less.

Of course there are situations where it's necessary or desirable to sell before your stock is long-term. There are also situations where it doesn't make a difference whether you hold long-term; for example, where you have a large capital loss that will swallow up all your gains, long-term and short-term.

Sometimes you have to choose between selling a short-term asset with a small gain and a long-term asset with a large gain. Selling the long-term asset will give you a lower rate, but the short-term asset will give you a smaller gain. There's no rule of thumb for resolving this conflict: you have to weigh the costs of each choice based on the particular facts of the situation.

Deferral. That's a boring word for a mundane concept: other things being equal, it's better to pay taxes later rather than sooner. The most obvious way to accomplish this is simply to avoid selling your winners. Even after your gains are long-term, it pays to delay sale—and taxes—from one year to the next. Wait until next year to sell and, if possible, the year after that. The sooner you sell your winners, the sooner Uncle Sam takes his bite.

This strategy is consistent with a tried and true investment strategy for accumulating wealth: buy and hold. People who sit on their stocks for long periods of time generally make out better than those who buy and sell frequently. But there are times when it's important to sell holdings, particularly to achieve diversification, as explained in Chapters 38 and 39.

Minimize gains. If you must sell a capital asset, it's usually best to minimize gains by selling assets with the highest basis. For example, you may have shares you acquired a long time ago for $15 and shares you acquired 18 months ago for $25. You're planning to sell some shares now at the current price of $30. With a little care, you can arrange to sell the newer shares and report a smaller gain. To do this, you may have to *identify* the shares you're selling, as explained in Chapter 50.

Avoid long-term losses. This rule of thumb goes against the grain of the buy-and-hold theory of investing. If you hold stock that has declined in value, you shouldn't rush to sell it simply to prevent the loss from becoming a long-term loss. Yet there are situations where a short-term loss is much better than a long-term loss.

For example, suppose you have plenty of capital gains, both short-term and long-term. You're planning to sell your XYZ stock, which is now trading at a $5,000 loss. If you sell while the loss is short-term, the loss will reduce your short-term gain, which is taxed at ordinary income tax rates. If you wait until the loss is long-term, it will reduce your long-term capital gain. In this situation, the short-term loss can save you as much as 35%, or $1,750, while the long-term loss saves you $750 at best.

Use large losses to soak up gains. If you have a large loss in one year, and also have stocks with gains, you don't have to worry about selling the gains right away because any unused loss will carry over to the next year. But suppose you're in the opposite situation. You have a large gain in one year, and stocks with large losses. In this situation, it may be to your advantage to sell the losing stock. The reason: capital losses carry *forward* but not *back*. You could end up paying tax on a large gain in Year 1, and be stuck with a large loss in some later year that you can't fully use because of the $3,000 limitation.

Protect long-term gains. Except in the situation described in the previous paragraph, it can be an advantage to prevent capital losses from reducing your long-term gains. You get more bang for your buck on a capital loss if it can be used against short-term gains or ordinary income rather than against your long-term gains. If you have a choice as to which year to sell losing stock and report a loss, it may be better to choose a year when you don't have long-term gains—unless the loss is so large it will otherwise go unused.

Chapter 6
Gift and Estate Tax 101

Equity compensation can result in wealth you never had before. As part of your personal financial planning, you should think about how it affects your estate plan. This isn't a do-it-yourself topic: estate planning should be done in consultation with a qualified professional. It helps if you know the basic rules of the game, though.

Gifts and Income Tax

Before we turn to gift and estate tax, let's take a look at how gifts affect your income tax.

Recipient doesn't report income. Gifts you receive aren't considered income. You don't report them on your income tax return in any way. There are two important qualifications on this simple rule.

- **True gifts.** This rule applies only to true gifts. You can't avoid paying income tax by calling something a gift when it isn't. For example, a "gift" you receive in exchange for services or some other consideration isn't a gift.

- **Income after gift.** If you receive a gift of property that produces income, you must report any income produced after the gift. For example, if you receive stock as a gift, you must report any dividends paid on that stock after the gift. There's an important exception for gifts of nonqualified options, described in Chapter 16.

No deduction except for charitable gifts. Some people hear that you can give $11,000 to a child "tax-free" and wonder if this means they can claim a deduction for such gifts. I'm afraid the answer is no. There is no deduction for gifts—except gifts to qualifying charities. The $11,000 limit applies to a *gift tax* exemption that's explained below. It has nothing to do with your *income tax*.

Basis and holding period. If the gift consists of property other than cash, the basis and holding period of the property will transfer to the recipient. It's important for the recipient to know when the donor acquired the property, the cost of the property, and any other information that would affect the property's basis. Ideally, the recipient of the gift should also receive records that will provide adequate proof of these facts.

It's also necessary to know the *value* of the property at the time of the gift. As donor, you need this information to determine whether the gift exceeds the $10,000 exclusion and, if so, the amount to report on the gift tax return. The recipient of the gift may also need this information to determine whether a deduction is available if the property is later sold at a loss.

Special rule for losses. If the property already had a loss at the time of the gift, the person receiving the gift can't deduct that loss on a later sale. Any loss deduction is limited to the amount the stock went down *after* the date of the gift. But for sales at a gain, the recipient can use the donor's basis.

Example: You bought stock for $10,000 and later gave it to your child when its value was $9,000. That means a $1,000 loss was "built-in" at the time of the gift. Your basis in the stock transfers to your child, but only for sales at a gain. If your child sells the stock for $8,500, the loss is only $500, even though you would have been able to deduct $1,500 if *you* had sold the stock. If your child sells the stock for $10,700, though, the gain is only $700, even though the stock went up $1,700 while your child held it. If your child sells the stock for a price between $9,000 (the value at the time of the gift) and $10,000 (the transferred basis), there is no gain or loss on the sale.

The holding period transfers, too. That means that if you held stock for more than a year before the gift, any sale by the recipient will produce long-term capital gain or loss— even if the recipient holds the stock for only a single day.

The Unified Transfer Tax

Federal estate and gift tax work hand in hand. Gifts you make during your lifetime can affect the amount of estate tax that's owed at your death.

To understand this, begin with the estate tax. This tax generally doesn't kick in until you leave more than $1,500,000 to someone other than your spouse or a charity. (The $1,500,000 figure applies to 2004 and 2005. That amount is scheduled to increase over the next several years with repeal of the estate tax taking place in 2010.*) The way this works is there is a *credit* that applies against the estate tax, to wipe out the tax that would otherwise apply to the first $1,500,000 of taxable estate.

This same credit is used against the gift tax. If you make a taxable gift, you don't actually pay tax on the gift unless the total amount of gifts in your lifetime is greater than $1,500,000. Because the same credit is used for both taxes—it's actually called the *unified credit*—any part of the credit that gets used up because of taxable gifts will reduce the amount of credit that's available for your estate when you die.

For wealthier individuals, it often makes sense to use the unified credit during their lifetime. But you don't want to use it unnecessarily if you think there's any chance your taxable estate will be more than $1,500,000. That's where the annual gift exclusion comes in.

---

* As things stand, the estate tax will spring back to life in 2011 unless Congress changes the law that was passed in 2001.

Annual Gift Exclusion

Under the gift tax you can give $11,000 per donee per year without reporting a taxable gift. (This is the 2004 amount. It's adjusted for inflation in $1,000 increments.) If you're married, you and your spouse can jointly give $22,000 per donee per year, even if the entire gift comes from just one of you. (To do this, you and your spouse must file gift tax returns and elect "gift-splitting.") You can use this rule to remove a large dollar amount of assets from your estate without incurring any gift tax or reducing your unified credit.

> **Example:** Suppose you're married and have three adult children, each of whom is married. Each year, you can give $22,000 to each child, and the spouse of each child, for total gifts of $132,000 per year without any gift tax implications.

This exclusion applies only to gifts of *present interests*. If you want to make your gift through a trust, you need to have an expert make certain the trust contains provisions that will prevent your gift from being a *future interest*. You can also make gifts of present interests through a Uniform Transfers to Minors Account, but these accounts are not well suited to transfers of large dollar amounts for various reasons.

Other Exclusions

The annual exclusion isn't the only way to make gifts without incurring gift tax. There's an unlimited exclusion for gifts to your spouse. (An annual limit applies if your spouse is not a United States citizen.) There's also an unlimited exclusion for the payment of medical expenses or educational costs, provided you make these payments directly to the service provider or educational institution.

Estate Planning

Estate planning is an exact science and a major industry. Even if you don't think you have to worry about estate tax, it's important to make certain your assets will pass in the way you intend, and avoid unnecessary probate costs. If there's a possibility the estate tax will apply—in many places, the cost of a good home and a reasonable life insurance policy will get you more than halfway there—it's important to see what can be done to prevent overpaying Uncle Sam. Estate tax rates are very high, and it's often possible to save tens of thousands, or even hundreds of thousands, with some relatively inexpensive trust arrangements and other planning techniques.

Part II
Stock Grants and Purchases

Most companies that provide equity compensation offer it in the form of *stock options,* or participation in an *employee stock purchase plan* (also called a *section 423 plan*). These types of equity compensation are covered in later parts of this book. In this part we look at the rules that apply when you acquire stock from your company *without* such arrangements.

Chapter 7 provides some terminology you need to get started. In Chapter 8 we look at rules that apply when you receive a stock grant or award from your company, or buy stock from the company. Rules explained in other parts of this book are based on rules in this chapter. Turn to Chapter 9 for planning ideas.

The tax rules for stock options are based on the rules described in these chapters. A quick skim of this part of the book may be helpful even if your compensation is in the form of options.

Part II
Stock Grants and Purchases

Chapter 7
Terminology for Stock Grants and Purchases

You need to know some tax lingo before you can read about stock grants and purchases. Here are the basic terms:

Stock grants and awards. If your company gives you stock without requiring payment from you (other than withholding), you've received a *stock grant*, also called a *stock award*. Other terms sometimes used include *restricted* stock and *founder's* stock.

Vested or not vested. Sometimes a company grants stock with no strings attached. You can sell the stock or keep it, and you don't give anything up if you stop working for the company. On the other hand, the company may insist that you earn the right to keep the stock. For example, the company may say that if you stop working for the company within a specified period, you forfeit the stock, or you have to sell it back to the company for the amount you originally paid.

These conditions can affect the tax consequences of receiving a stock grant, or buying stock from your company. We have one set of rules for when the stock is *vested*, and another for when the stock is *not vested*. Generally, your stock is *vested* if you can sell it, or if you can keep the stock (or at least get full value for it) when you stop working for the company. If both conditions are absent (in other words, you can't sell the stock, and you'll either forfeit it or sell it back for less than full value if you leave your job), the stock is *not vested*.

Example: Your company grants you 500 shares of stock, but you'll forfeit the stock if you stop working for the company within the next year. The stock isn't *vested* until the year is up.

For most purposes you're the owner of the stock even before it's vested. For example, unless you've agreed otherwise, you have the right to vote as a shareholder and to receive any dividends that are declared and paid during that period. As you'll see in the following chapters, the tax law treats you as if you don't own the stock until it vests, unless you file the *section 83b election*, described below.

Substantial risk of forfeiture. If the company imposes conditions that prevent your stock from being vested, the stock is *subject to a substantial risk of forfeiture*. That's quite a mouthful, and all it means is that the stock isn't vested, so I try to avoid using this term. I mention it here in case you see it somewhere else and wonder where it fits in.

Section 83b election. When you receive stock that isn't vested, you can actually choose which of two sets of tax rules will apply to you. One set of tax rules applies if you do nothing, and a different set of rules applies if you file a *section 83b election*. This is a statement you file with the IRS *within 30 days after you receive the stock* saying that you want the alternate set of tax rules to apply. The following chapters explain the effects of this election.

> ▪ You can find more details concerning vesting and the section 83b election in Part VIII.

Chapter 8
Rules for Stock Grants and Purchases

This is the most important chapter of this book. It lays the foundation for nearly everything else we discuss: non-qualified options, incentive stock options and employee stock purchase plans. We'll refer back to this chapter when we cover those topics. For now, however, we're concerned only with simple transactions where your company either sells stock to you (at full value or at a bargain price), or gives you a stock grant or award.

> • **Tax trap alert.** You may not think you need to worry about the tax consequences if you pay full value for stock you receive from your company. Think again. If the stock isn't vested at the time of purchase, your failure to make a section 83b election, as explained later, could be costly.

Stock grants and stock purchases. We can cover the tax treatment of stock grants and stock purchases together because the rules are exactly the same. You can think of a stock grant as a purchase for zero dollars. Whenever we refer to the amount paid for the stock, that amount is zero in the case of a stock grant or award. (See rules in Part IX if you buy under an employee stock purchase plan.)

Three sets of rules. There are different rules for each of the following three situations:

- Your stock is *vested* when you receive it.

- Your stock is *not vested* when you receive it.

- Your stock is *not vested* when you receive it, and you file the *section 83b election*.

Generally your stock is *vested* if you can keep it (or sell it for full value) when your employment terminates. See Part VIII for details on vesting and making the section 83b election.

Stock Is Vested

When you receive vested stock, you have to report compensation income for the year you receive it. The amount of income is the fair market value of the stock at the time you received it, reduced by the amount you paid for it, if any.

Example: You receive a stock grant worth $20,000. The stock is vested when you receive it. You have to report $20,000 of compensation income in addition to all your other compensation and non-compensation income for that year.

Example: You buy $20,000 worth of stock from your company for $15,000. The stock is vested when you receive it. You have to report $5,000 of compensation income in addition to all your other compensation and non-compensation income for that year.

Cashless income. Some people tend to associate *income* with *cash*. That isn't the case here. You have to report income, and pay tax, *even if you haven't sold the stock*. You didn't receive any cash—in fact, you may have paid cash to receive the stock—yet you have to come up with money to pay the IRS. Careful planning is essential!

The amount of tax you'll pay depends on your tax bracket. If the entire amount falls in the 28% bracket in the second example above, you'll pay 28% of $5,000, or $1,400 (plus any social security tax, self-employment tax or state income tax). If your bargain element is large, it's likely that some of the income will push up into a higher tax bracket than your usual one.

No capital gain. You may have capital gain later when you sell the stock. But the income you report now, when you receive the stock, is compensation income, not capital gain. Don't be confused by the fact that your compensation is in the form of stock.

Withholding. If you're an employee, the company is required to withhold on this compensation income. Of course the IRS insists on receiving withholding payments in cash, not in shares of stock. There are various ways the company can handle the withholding requirement. The most common one is simply to require you to pay the withholding amount in cash at the time you receive the stock.

> **Example:** You purchase 1,000 shares of your company's stock for $15 per share when they're worth $40 per share. The stock is vested when you receive it. Your purchase price is $15,000 and your compensation income is $25,000. In addition to the purchase price, the company requires you to pay $9,000 to cover state and federal withholding requirements.

The amount paid must cover federal and state income tax withholding, and the employee share of social security tax as well. The portion that is income tax withholding will be a credit against the tax you owe when you file your return at the end of the year. Be prepared: the amount of withholding won't necessarily be large enough to cover the full amount of the tax due on this income. You may end up owing tax on April 15 even if you paid withholding at the time you exercised the option, because the withholding amount is merely an estimate of the actual tax liability.

> **Example:** You receive a stock grant valued at $10,000 and pay $2,500 in federal withholding. Depending on your tax bracket and other factors, the actual tax on this $10,000 of income may be as much as $3,500, which means you could end up

owing more (or getting a smaller refund) on
April 15.

> - Withholding you pay when you receive your stock is
>   *not* part of the purchase price. Don't include
>   withholding in your basis when you sell the stock.

Non-employees. If you're not an employee, withholding won't apply when you receive the stock. The
income should be reported to you on Form 1099-MISC
instead of Form W-2. Remember that this is compensation for services. In general this income will be subject
to self-employment tax as well as federal and state
income tax.

Tax consequences when you sell the stock. When you
sell the stock, you're treated the same as if you had
bought it on the date the company gave it to you, for an
amount equal to the amount you paid (if any) *plus the
amount of income you reported.* Even if you didn't
actually pay anything for the stock, you have *basis* equal
to the amount of income you reported. It's as if the
company paid you that much cash and then you used the
cash to buy the stock. If you sell the stock after holding it
for a year or less, you'll have a short-term capital gain or
loss on the sale. If you hold it for more than a year, your
gain or loss will be long-term. It's important to keep a
record of when you received the stock, the amount (if
any) you paid for it and the amount of income you
reported at that time.

> **Example:** You buy 1,000 shares of stock at $20 per
> share when the value is $50 per share. The stock is
> vested when you receive it, and you report $30,000
> of compensation income. Fifteen months later you
> sell the stock for $60,000. Your basis includes the
> $20,000 you paid plus the $30,000 you reported as
> compensation income. The sale produces a
> $10,000 long-term capital gain.

Stock Is Not Vested

If the stock isn't vested when you buy it, you have a choice of two different tax treatments. First we'll look at what happens under the general rule. Then we'll see what happens if you file a *section 83b election.*

Under the general rule, receiving stock that isn't vested is a pretty simple event. You report nothing at all at that time. You may *feel* richer if you didn't pay for the stock, or you bought it at a bargain price, but the tax law says you aren't richer until the stock vests. It isn't regular income, or AMT income, or even tax-exempt income. It's nothing at all. Your only obligation at this point is to maintain a record of what stock you acquired, when you received it and the amount (if any) you paid, so you can report the proper consequences later.

Dividends before vesting. You own the stock while you're waiting for it to vest, so you may receive dividends during this period. Yet the tax law treats you as if you don't own the stock yet, so the company won't report these payments as dividends. Any dividends you receive during this period are treated as *compensation.* The company will report them on your W-2, *not* on Form 1099-DIV. That means they won't qualify for the new 15% rate that applies to most dividend income. You get the benefit of that special tax rate only for dividends paid after the stock vests.

Tax consequences at vesting. If all goes well, you'll stay with the company long enough to own the stock outright. At that point—when the stock vests—you'll report compensation income equal to the difference between the fair market value of the stock and the amount (if any) you paid for it. In this case, *fair market value is determined on the vesting date.* If the value of the stock goes up while you're waiting for the stock to vest, you'll end up reporting that added value as compensation income when the stock vests.

Example: Your company lets you buy $10,000 worth of stock for $8,000. If your employment terminates within the following two years, you have to sell the stock back to the company for $8,000, the amount you paid. That means your stock isn't vested. You don't file the section 83b election, so you have no income to report in the year of purchase.

Two years later you're still working for the company and the stock vests. At that time the stock is worth $15,000. You report $7,000 of compensation income: the current value of $15,000 minus your cost of $8,000.

> ▪ **The *Alves* trap.** You can have a restriction that prevents your stock from being vested even if you pay full value for the stock. Because of a tax case called *Alves*, you may end up paying unnecessary tax in this situation. If the stock goes up in value before it vests, you'll have to report that increase as compensation income at that time. You can avoid this result by filing the section 83b election as explained below.

Tax consequences at sale. A sale of the stock after it's vested will result in capital gain or loss. Your basis will be the amount you paid for the stock plus the amount of income you reported at the time the stock became vested. Your gain or loss will be long-term if you held the stock more than a year after the *vesting date*. Otherwise any gain or loss will be short-term.

> **Example:** Let's continue with the previous example. Six months after the stock vests, you sell it for $20,000. You paid only $8,000 for the stock, but you reported $7,000 of income when the stock vested, so your basis for the stock is $15,000. You report only $5,000 of gain on the sale. Your gain is short-term, even though you held the stock 2½ years, because for tax purposes you're treated as if you acquired the stock on the date it vested.

Tax consequences of forfeiture. It's possible that you'll stop working for the company before the stock vests, and forfeit the stock or have to sell it back for the amount you paid for it—or less. If you sell it back for the same amount you paid to receive the stock, you report no gain or loss. You may feel that you've lost something, because the stock was worth more than you received in the forced sale. But you never included anything in income for that added value, so you can't reduce your income for the loss you suffered. You get no deduction in this situation.

> **Example:** We'll use the previous example one more time. You bought stock worth $10,000 for $8,000, but you reported no income at the time because the stock wasn't vested. Before the stock vested, you left to work for another company and had to sell the stock back for the same $8,000 you originally paid, even though the stock was worth much more. You should report the sale on your tax return, but you have no gain or loss, so it doesn't affect the amount of tax you pay.

If you sell the stock back for *less than* $8,000, you'll report a capital loss.

Section 83b Election

You can change the consequences described above by filing a *section 83b election*. You send a notice to the IRS that includes certain information and declares that you want this election to apply. *This election must be filed within 30 days after you receive the stock.* See Chapter 33 for details on making this election.

If you make the section 83b election, you're treated as if the stock were vested when you received it:

- You report compensation income at the time you receive the stock, measured by the value of the stock at that time. When you determine the value of the stock for this purpose, you have to ignore the existence of any temporary restriction. If the amount you pay is equal to the fair market value of the stock, the amount of income you report is zero.

- Dividends you receive before the stock vests will *not* be treated as compensation income.

- You have nothing to report at the time the stock vests.

- When you sell the stock, your basis is the amount (if any) you paid for the stock plus the amount of income you reported when you received it. Your holding period goes back to that date, too, so any gain or loss will be long-term if more than a year has elapsed from that date.

> ▪ By far the biggest problem with the section 83b election is missing the 30-day deadline. You can't wait until you file your tax return to make this election. You have to do it right away.

Tax consequences of forfeiture. It might seem logical to get a deduction if you forfeit stock after making the section 83b election. After all, you voluntarily reported income and paid tax as a result of making this election. A corresponding deduction when you forfeit the stock would make sense. Unfortunately, the law says you can't claim a deduction in this situation. Possibly this rule is designed to prevent people from using the section 83b election to manipulate their income in an artificial way. Whatever the reason, the law is clear: no deduction for a forfeiture.

> ▪ Before making the section 83b election, be sure you consider the risk that you may forfeit the stock and receive no deduction relative to the income you reported at the time of the election.

Tax consequences of vesting. If you make the section 83b election, there is no tax consequence at the time the stock vests. Under this election you're treated as if the stock was vested when you acquired it, so there is nothing to report at the time it *actually* becomes vested.

Tax consequences at sale. You have the same tax consequences for a sale of stock after a section 83b election as if the stock had been vested when you received it. Your holding period begins on the date you received the stock, and your basis is the amount paid for the stock (if any), increased by the amount of compensation income you reported at that time.

Chapter 9
Planning for Stock Grants and Purchases

Most tax planning for stock grants and purchases revolves around the section 83b election. Even if your company offers stock that will be vested when you receive it, you may wish to consider whether you can change the deal and use the section 83b election to reduce your taxes.

Some of these planning ideas require cooperation from the company. You should bear in mind that good tax planning for you may be bad tax planning for the company. Anything you do to reduce or postpone the amount of compensation income you have to report will cause a corresponding decrease or delay in the amount of compensation deduction the company will enjoy.

Accelerating Income

Suppose you have the following deal with your employer. You'll receive 100 shares of stock without restrictions if your employment continues for another year. This is just a stock grant without restriction as described in Chapter 8. In some circumstances you can improve on the tax consequences without really changing the deal.

Consider an alternative where you receive the stock *now* instead of having to wait a year—but you'll forfeit the stock if your employment terminates before a year is up. Basically that's the same as the other deal: you get to keep the stock only if you work for that company for a year. You may get a better tax treatment, however, if you make the section 83b election. That would permit you to report compensation income at the time you receive the stock, rather than at the end of the year when the stock vests.

You would do this only if two things are true. First, you expect the value of the stock to go up during that year. There's no point reporting income earlier than necessary just for the sake of paying taxes sooner. If the stock is going up, though, you can use this maneuver to reduce the amount of compensation income you have to report. It may make sense to negotiate this change if you expect a big increase in the stock's value in the near future.

In addition, unless the value of the stock is very small when you receive it, you would want to be pretty confident that your employment will last through the year before heading in this direction. You wouldn't feel smart if you made this change, and paid taxes after filing the section 83b election, only to find that you end up forfeiting the stock.

> **Example:** Your employer offers to reward you with 2,000 shares of stock if you continue to work there another year. You feel that the value of the stock is likely to go up in that time, so you suggest an alternative: you'll receive the stock *now*, but *forfeit* it if you don't continue to work there another year. The company agrees. You receive the stock, make the section 83b election and pay tax on the current value.
>
> Then the unexpected happens. You get an offer you can't refuse from another company. You quit your current job and forfeit the stock. Economically, you're in the same position as if you hadn't made the change, because you wouldn't have received the stock under the original deal. From a tax standpoint though, you're worse off, because you reported income when you made the section 83b election and you won't get any offsetting deduction when you forfeit the stock.

Deferring Income

You can also use the rules for vesting to postpone income. Suppose your company is going to make a stock grant to you, without any restrictions. Normally that would mean you'll report compensation income, but you want to avoid reporting income this year. In this situation you might want to consider *asking* for a restriction on the stock, so that you'll forfeit it if your employment ends within the next year.

Naturally, you would do this only if you're confident that your employment will in fact continue for that period of time. You could be forfeiting a valuable right if you accept such a restriction and you leave your job. In addition, it wouldn't make sense to do this if you anticipate a great increase in the value of the stock while you're waiting for it to vest. These two possibilities—forfeiting the stock or seeing a hefty increase in its value before vesting—make delayed vesting a risky planning device. In limited circumstances, though, it makes sense to at least consider this approach.

You may be tempted to use a very short time period for the stock to vest. For example, if you're going to receive a stock grant in November, you may want to delay vesting until the beginning of January. That's a risky proposition, though. You can delay reporting compensation only if there is a *substantial risk of forfeiture*. The IRS might decide this wasn't *substantial*. There's no specific time period that's safe, but I get nervous with vesting that occurs less than six months after receipt of the stock. Similarly, anything else you do to reduce or eliminate the risk that you'll forfeit the stock may cast doubt on whether the tax deferral will pass muster.

Benefits and Risks of Section 83b Election

The section 83b election can provide multiple benefits. Most obviously, it reduces the amount of compensation income you have to report if the value of your stock goes up during the vesting period. It also starts the clock running sooner for long-term capital gains. This can be to your benefit even if the stock's value doesn't go up during the vesting period, assuming it goes up afterward and you sell it in the year following vesting.

Example: You receive stock with vesting delayed by one year and make the section 83b election. A year later, the value is unchanged, so you didn't avoid any compensation income by making the election. But six months later the stock has gone up and you sell it. Because of the section 83b election, you'll report long-term capital gain. Without the election, your holding period would have started when the stock vested, and you would have had short-term capital gain when you sold the stock.

There's another benefit if the stock pays dividends. We mentioned earlier that dividends paid before the stock vests are treated as compensation income. If you make the section 83b election, you're treated as if you received vested shares. That means any dividends are eligible for the new 15% tax rate.

There's a downside to the election. For one thing, it requires you to pay tax earlier than would otherwise be necessary. All other things being equal, it's better to pay taxes later. You also have to consider the possibility the stock value will *fall* during the vesting period, in which case the election caused you to pay more tax than necessary. And then there's the possibility of a real disaster: paying tax after making the section 83b election and then forfeiting the stock. You didn't just pay tax sooner in this situation. You paid a tax you never would have had to pay at all!

There are some circumstances where you should definitely make the section 83b election. One is where you paid fair market value for the stock, but agreed to have it be subject to a restriction that prevents it from being vested. There's no cost at all to this election, and it can prevent you from having a painful tax bill at the time the stock vests. It's also a good idea to think about the section 83b election in situations where the value of the stock is very low at the time you receive it, and there's a possibility it will rise sharply before vesting. This is often the case when a company is preparing to issue stock in an initial public offering (IPO).

Part III
Options in General

This part of the book provides essential information for working with both nonqualified options and incentive stock options. Chapter 10 provides an overview of how options work and introduces you to option terminology. Chapter 11 describes what happens when you receive an option, and what you should do at that time. Chapter 12 explains the difference between nonqualified stock options and incentive stock options, and how to determine which you have. Finally, Chapter 13 takes you step by step through the process of exercising an option.

Part III
Options in General

Chapter 10
Options 101

A stock option is an agreement providing terms under which you can buy a specified number of shares of stock at a specified price. Your option will increase in value as the company's stock grows. If the stock goes down instead, you won't reap value from your option but you won't have lost anything, because you aren't *required* to buy stock. A stock option is that free lunch you've been looking for: a chance to benefit from the upside without any risk of loss on the downside.

Option Terminology

Stock options have their own lingo. Here are the basic terms you need to understand.

- **Grant or award.** You receive the stock option when the company makes a *grant* or *award*.

- **Vesting.** The option agreement or plan may say you can't use the option right away. The time you have to wait before using the option is the *vesting period*. An option is *vested* when you can use the option to buy stock.

- **Exercise.** You *exercise* an option when you notify the company that you want to purchase stock and provide payment according to the terms of the option.

- **Exercise price.** This is the price you pay if you decide to exercise the option. If you have an option to buy 100 shares at $15 per share, your exercise price is $15 per share. The exercise price is also sometimes called the *strike price*, the *striking price* or the *option price*.

- **Spread.** The difference between the current value of the stock and the strike price is the *spread*. If the current value of the stock is $20 and your option permits you to buy it at $15, the spread is $5 per share. The spread is also sometimes called the *bargain element*.

- **In the money.** An option is *in the money* when the spread is positive—in other words, when the value of the stock is higher than the exercise price.

- **Under water.** Options are *under water* (or *out of the money*) if the spread is negative; in other words, if the strike price is higher than the current value of the stock. There is no special tax significance to an option being under water, but the practical significance is that the option will not become valuable until the stock price recovers.

- **Option agreement.** When a company grants an option, it should provide you with an *option agreement*. This document spells out the key terms of your option, including the number of shares you can buy, the purchase price, and the time periods during which you're permitted to exercise the option.

- **Stock option plan.** Options are usually (but not always) issued pursuant to a formal *stock option plan* adopted by the board of directors and approved by the shareholders. The stock option plan often provides additional details concerning the terms of your options. Don't confuse the stock option plan with a prospectus or other summary. You need a copy of the plan itself to know precisely what your rights are.

- **Prospectus.** An option is an opportunity to invest, so it's appropriate for the company to provide a *prospectus* when granting options. This is a summary of the terms of the option and other information intended to help you decide whether to exercise the option.

> ▪ It's *very important* to keep good records concerning equity compensation in general and stock options in particular. You should have a safe place where you keep your option agreement and a copy of the stock option plan. Keep any prospectus or other information materials, too. In a pinch, all of these documents may be useful in determining your rights.

More on Option Vesting

The words *vesting* and *vested* cause plenty of confusion. Partly this is because they're used differently depending on whether we're talking about *stock* or *stock options*. We say *stock* is vested at the point in time when you can quit your job and still keep the stock (or at least receive full value for it). Part VIII of this book deals with various rules for vesting of stock.

We mean something different when we say an *option* is vested. An option becomes vested at the point in time when you can exercise it (use it to buy stock). You don't necessarily get to keep an option when you quit your job, even if the option is vested. Most options terminate when your employment terminates or shortly thereafter, perhaps with some added leeway if your employment ends due to death or disability.

> ▪ Your option may be vested (exercisable) even though the stock you buy under the option is *not* vested. If your company has an "early exercise" stock option plan (see Chapter 24), you may be in a position where you can exercise the option but you don't get to keep the stock if your employment terminates before a specified date.

The vesting rules for your stock option may appear in the option agreement or in the stock option plan. One of the first things you should do when you receive a stock option is determine when it becomes exercisable—in other words, when it vests. Many options vest gradually over a number of years.

> **Example:** You receive an option with a ten-year term, permitting you to buy 120 shares of your company's stock at a specified price. The option has a four-year vesting schedule. For the first year you can't exercise any of the option. Beginning on the first anniversary of the grant date, you can exercise 25% of the option. In other words, you can buy up to 30 shares. When you reach the second anniversary of the grant date, you can buy another 30 shares. Vesting is cumulative, so if you didn't buy the first 30 shares yet, you're now eligible to buy 60 shares. After four years have gone by, you're eligible to buy all 120 shares. You can exercise the entire option then, or part of it, or wait until later.

Option Economics

Suppose you hold an option to buy 1,000 shares of XYZ stock at $15 per share. The stock is trading at $20. What is the value of your option?

Many people make the mistake of saying the option has a value of $5,000. True, that's what you would receive if you exercised the option and immediately sold the stock. But the option is surely worth more than that.

An option has two kinds of value. One is called *intrinsic value,* and that is what the $5,000 represents. The other part of the value of an option is called the *time value.*

Consider the situation where you hold an option with no intrinsic value. The strike price is $20, and that's the current trading price, too. Is that option worthless, just because the spread is zero?

Certainly not. The option gives you an opportunity to obtain a bargain any time in the future if the stock's price goes up. Meanwhile, you aren't at risk of losing anything if the stock's price goes down. An option gives you the opportunity to profit from the upside without risking loss on the downside. That's a beautiful thing! It's the reason an option has value even if the spread is zero.

> - Complicated mathematical formulas are used to determine the value of stock options. Among other variables, they take into account prevailing interest rates, the term of the option, the current price of the stock, and the stock's *volatility* (a measure of how much the price of this particular stock tends to zigzag up and down). Chapter 40 provides details.

Chapter 11
Receiving Stock Options

Most nonqualified options, and *all* incentive stock options, are granted pursuant to a *stock option plan* that was adopted by the company's board of directors and approved by the shareholders. The board of directors, or a committee appointed by the board (usually called the *compensation committee*), may decide who receives the awards and the specific terms of the options. In some cases options are granted according to a formula set forth in the plan or in an employment agreement.

What You'll Receive

When a company grants an option it should provide certain documents. You should receive an *option agreement*, setting forth the specific terms of your option. If the option is issued under a plan, you may also receive a copy of the plan, which provides some general rules that govern all options. In many cases the company provides a summary of the plan, called a *prospectus*.

Make sure you keep these documents in a safe place. You should review them from time to time for planning purposes. At a minimum, you want to think about your options before the end of each year to determine whether to exercise some or all of the options by December 31 as part of your tax planning.

> ■ **Note:** It's a good idea to get a copy of the stock option plan if it's available, because this document can clarify your rights in some situations.

Typical Terms

Companies have great flexibility in the terms they can offer for options. Your options may differ from the typical option in a number of important ways. Yet it may be helpful to compare your option with the norm:

- The exercise price is usually set at (or near) the value of the stock at the time the option is granted. For incentive stock options, the price *must* be greater than or equal to the fair market value of the stock when the option is granted.

- The option becomes exercisable over a period of several years. For example, you may be able to exercise 25% after one year, 50% after two years, and so on. This is not a requirement, and some options are fully exercisable when issued.

- Cash payment is usually required at the time of exercise, but some companies make a form of "cashless exercise" available, arranging for a loan from a broker.

- The option expires ten years after it was issued, or earlier if employment terminates. You may or may not have a grace period (usually no more than three months) to exercise options at the time employment terminates. The grace period generally applies only to options that were exercisable when your employment terminated. Options that were scheduled to become exercisable on some later date typically expire when your employment ends, even if the date they would have become exercisable falls within the grace period.

Tax Consequences of Receiving an Option

With rare exceptions, there's no tax to pay, and nothing to report, at the time you receive a nonqualified option. The exceptions:

- You receive an option that's actively traded on an established securities market, or virtually identical to options that are actively traded. In many years of experience with options, I've never seen this rule apply.

- You receive a nonqualified option that's "in the money" to such a great extent at the time you receive it that the option is considered equivalent to owning the stock. For example, at a time when the stock is worth $40 per share you receive an option that permits you to buy the stock for $2 per share. This rule wouldn't apply to a nonqualified option that's only slightly in the money—for example, a nonqualified option with an exercise price of $35 that's issued when the stock value is $40. (ISOs *can't* be in the money when issued.)

In all other cases you have nothing to report at the time you receive an option. This is true even if the option is fully vested when you receive it.

No Section 83b Election

There's persistent confusion among taxpayers—and even among some tax professionals—about the section 83b election. This election can provide tax savings when you receive *stock* that's not vested. But the election doesn't apply when you receive an *option* except in the unusual situation where it's a publicly traded option. You may hear that there's an election you can make to reduce your tax when you receive a nonqualified option, but that's a mistake. The section 83b election is for stock only.*

No Tax When Option Becomes Exercisable

You may receive an option that isn't immediately exercisable. You're permitted to exercise the option only

---

* This may include stock you receive when you exercise an option.

if you continue to work for the company for a stated period.

> **Example:** You receive an option to buy 300 shares of the company's stock, but you're not permitted to exercise the option immediately. If you're still employed with that company a year later you become eligible to exercise half of this option. After another year of employment the option is fully exercisable.

The dates on which the option becomes exercisable are obviously significant, but you don't report income on these dates. The tax law takes no notice of them.

Tax Planning Starts Now

Tax planning for your options should begin the day you receive them. Begin by understanding your rights under the agreement and the stock option plan. Read these documents carefully, and make sure you can answer these questions:

- What is the earliest date you can exercise the option? Does it become exercisable in stages?

- What do you need to do when you exercise the option? Can you borrow to exercise the option? Can you pay the exercise price using stock you already own?

- What restrictions will be imposed on the stock you receive when you exercise the option? Can you sell it right away if you want to? Transfer it to a trust or family partnership? Does the company have the right to get the stock back under any circumstances?

- When will the option terminate? Can you exercise after your employment terminates? What if you die while holding the option?

Start thinking *now* about how and when you'll exercise the options. Will you exercise them all at once, or in stages over a number of years? What scenario will provide the best result for you? How will you come up with the money to exercise the options? And the money to pay the taxes? How will you handle an unexpected situation, such as loss of your job?

Chapter 12
Nonqualified Options and ISOs

Options you receive as compensation for services come in two flavors: *nonqualified options* and *incentive stock options*. If you're an employee, you may receive either type of option, or some of each. If you're not an employee, you can only receive nonqualified options. An option granted to a non-employee, such as an independent director or consultant, can't be an ISO.

Differences in Tax Treatment

Employees generally prefer incentive stock options. The special tax rules for ISOs are favorable to the holders of these options:

- You have to report income when you exercise a nonqualified option, but not when you exercise an incentive stock option.

- The income you report when you exercise a nonqualified option is compensation income. If you satisfy a special holding period requirement after exercising an incentive stock option, all your profit from the ISO will be long-term capital gain. You won't have to report any compensation income.

But ISOs bring bad news, too. When you exercise an incentive stock option, you're likely to have to pay alternative minimum tax (AMT). This tax may take away much of the benefit of not having to report income when you exercise your option. Apart from the cost of paying the tax, the complexity of dealing with the AMT can be daunting.

ISOs may be unattractive to employers for other reasons. Options don't qualify as incentive stock options unless they meet a list of requirements set forth in the Internal Revenue Code. Employers have more flexibility in dealing with nonqualified options. What's more, employers receive less favorable tax treatment for ISOs than for nonqualified options. The tax detriment to the company from choosing incentive stock options instead of nonqualified options may be greater than the tax benefit to the employee.

Which Do You Have?

Sometimes option holders are uncertain as to which type of option they have. This is the first thing you need to know! If you're unclear on this, here's how to find out.

Non-employees. If you're not an employee—in other words, you're not someone who has withholding taken from each paycheck and receives a W-2 at the end of the year—your option *has* to be a nonqualified option. The tax law doesn't permit companies to issue incentive stock options to non-employees. Even if your option says it's an ISO, it's a nonqualified option if you aren't an employee.

The option agreement. If you're an employee and unsure which type of option you have, the most reliable way to find the answer is to read the option agreement. You should have a copy of this document in your permanent records. If you don't, be sure to obtain a copy from the company.

- If the option agreement says the option is not an ISO, then that's your answer. Even if an option meets all other requirements to be an incentive stock option, the tax law says it's not an ISO if the option agreement declares that the option isn't an incentive stock option.

- If the option agreement says the option is an incentive stock option, then that *should* be your answer. Just saying that an option is an ISO isn't enough to make it one, however. The option has to satisfy a list of requirements in the tax law. For example, ISOs must be issued pursuant to a plan that has been approved by the company's shareholders. An incentive stock option can't be issued for a price that's lower than the fair market value of the stock on the date the option is granted, and can't extend for a period of more than 10 years. There are additional requirements, including special restrictions for individuals who own more than 10% of the stock of the company issuing the options.

Other rules. There are other rules that can change an incentive stock option to a nonqualified option. One is a $100,000 per year limit on the amount of incentive stock options you can receive. The limit applies to the year the option becomes *exercisable,* not the year you receive the option. But the limit is based on the value of the stock at the time the option is granted.

> **Example:** You receive an incentive stock option that permits you to buy up to $400,000 worth of the company's stock. You can exercise one-fourth of the option immediately, but have to wait a year before exercising the second one-fourth, another year for the third one-fourth and one more year for the final one-fourth. This arrangement complies with the $100,000 limit, even if the stock is worth millions by the time you're eligible to exercise the last one-fourth.

The option described in the example consumes your entire limit for a four-year period. If you received any other options that became exercisable during that period, they would have to be nonqualified options.

Sometimes a company will issue options that exceed the limit without specifying that part of the option is a nonqualified option. That means you could have an option that *says* it's an ISO when in reality it's partly or entirely a nonqualified option. It's important to know how much of your option is nonqualified in this situation, because this will have great influence on your tax planning.

Termination of employment. The tax law says an option isn't an ISO if you exercise it more than a limited period after your employment terminates: one year if employment terminates because of disability, otherwise three months. Your option, or the plan under which it's issued, may provide a *shorter* period. If your ISO remains exercisable for a *longer* period, its status as an ISO will terminate at the end of the three-month period.

Changing the agreement. Sometimes companies and option holders agree to change the terms of the options after they've been granted. If the option is an ISO, these changes have to be carefully reviewed. Some types of changes will be treated as a cancellation of the old option and issuance of a new one. The "new" option won't qualify as an incentive stock option if it doesn't meet all applicable requirements. In particular, it would be necessary to increase the exercise price if the value of the stock went up after the original issue date of the option. Great care is necessary whenever changing the terms of an incentive stock option that's already been issued.

Chapter 13
How to Exercise a Stock Option

In the rest of this book we'll talk about *when* to exercise options, and what your tax consequences will be. Before that knowledge can do you any good, you need to know *how* to exercise a stock option.

Step 1: Know your rights. To start with, you need to know whether you can exercise any of your stock options, and if so, which ones. Read your option agreement and relevant parts of the stock option plan. If you don't have copies of these documents, you should obtain them from the company.

You may find that you can exercise some of your stock options but not others. As indicated above, you may be able to exercise only *part* of a stock option. Even if your stock options are fully exercisable, you may wish to exercise only part of an option. Most plans permit partial exercise, subject to a minimum amount.

Example: A typical provision might say you can exercise part of an option, but no fewer than ten shares at a time unless that's all you have at the time you exercise.

Step 2: Select a stock option. You may find that you have more than one stock option that's available for exercise. Unless you're planning to exercise all your options at once, you need to choose which stock option to exercise.

Example: You hold an option to buy 100 shares at $18 per share, and another option to buy 200 shares at $15 per share. Both stock options are fully exercisable. You want to exercise for 100 shares.

The easy thing to do is to exercise the option for 100 shares at $18. But if your plan permits, you can exercise half of the other option instead. That would cost $300 less because of the lower exercise price, but cause you to report an additional $300 of income.

At one time, the tax rules said you had to exercise incentive stock options in the same order you received them. Under this *sequential exercise rule*, if you hadn't exercised your oldest ISO, you couldn't exercise any other ISO. This rule is long gone. Unless your company has an outdated plan, you can exercise your options in any order.

Step 3: Select a method of payment. In the bad old days there was only one way to pay for stock when you exercised an option. In legal mumbo-jumbo, you had to *tender readily available funds*. In other words, you had to come up with cash.

That's still a popular method of payment, but some companies now make other alternatives available. The company may have an arrangement with a stock broker under which some or all of the stock is sold immediately to cover the exercise price and any tax withholding. See below for a discussion of *cashless exercise*.

Another possibility is to use stock you already own to pay the exercise price. For example, if it will cost $2,000 to exercise your option, you can turn in $2,000 worth of stock instead of $2,000 in cash. Not all companies offer this alternative. You may achieve benefits with this form of exercise that aren't available when you pay cash. Due to the complexity involved, Part VI of this book devotes several chapters to this form of exercise.

Step 4: Withholding. If you're an employee and you exercise a nonqualified option, the company has to withhold on the income you receive from exercising the option (see Chapter 48). Usually that means you have to come up with additional cash besides the option price.

Before you exercise your option, you should determine what your withholding obligation will be and how you'll meet it. The precise dollar amount won't be determined until you exercise the option, because the amount of income (and therefore the amount of withholding) is based on the value of the stock on the day you exercise.

Step 5: Exercise the option. Now you know exactly what you want to do and you're ready to exercise the option. Once again you have to look at the option agreement and the stock option plan to learn how to proceed. Most larger companies have a form you must fill out when you exercise an option. Other companies simply require notification in writing. In that case you would write a brief letter or memo something like this:

> *In accordance with my option agreement dated September 10, 1998 I hereby exercise my option to purchase 120 shares of common stock at the price of $30 per share. My check in the amount of $3,600 is attached.*

Chances are you won't be the first person to exercise an option at your company. If you're in doubt as to how to proceed, contact the appropriate office for instructions.

Cashless Exercise

Some employers make it easier for option holders to exercise their options by providing a way to combine the exercise of the option with a sale of some or all of the stock. In this situation you don't have to come up with any money to exercise the option or pay any withholding. That's why we call this a *cashless exercise* of your option.

Usually the company makes arrangements with a brokerage firm, which loans the money needed to buy the stock. The brokerage firm sells some or all of the stock immediately, with part of the proceeds being used to repay the loan as soon as the sale proceeds become available. Another part of the sale proceeds will be used to cover any withholding requirement that applies, and any brokerage commissions and other fees. You receive whatever is left in the form of cash or unsold shares.

Not all companies permit this method of exercise. Some companies want to encourage option holders to retain the stock so they'll have an ongoing stake in the business. Others may be concerned that sales executed in this manner will depress the price of their stock. Review your option documents, or check with the company, to see if this method of exercising your options is available.

Tax consequences. The tax consequences of a cashless exercise are the same as if you took two separate steps: exercising the option, then selling the stock. The fact that you did both at once has no particular significance. Any gain or loss on your sale will be short-term, of course. In the case of an incentive stock option, you'll have an early (disqualifying) disposition.

Frequently asked questions. Most confusion in this area comes when people don't realize that the single act of choosing a cashless exercise has to be reported as two transactions.

Q: My gain from exercising the option appears on my Form W-2 as wages—but Form 1099-B reports the full amount of proceeds, including the gain. Why is the same amount reported twice?

A: The same amount is *reported* twice, but it isn't *taxed* twice. Form 1099-B shows how much you received for selling the stock. When you figure your gain or loss, the amount reported on your W-2 is treated as an additional amount paid for the stock. (In other words, it increases your *basis*.) The effect is to reduce your gain or increase your loss, so you're not double taxed.

Q: Why do I have gain or loss when the stock was sold at the same time I exercised?

A: Often there's a gain or loss to report, for two reasons. First, the amount reported on your

W-2 as income is usually based on the stock's average price for the day you exercised your option, but the broker may have sold at a price slightly (or more than slightly) above or below that average price. And second, your sale proceeds are likely to be reduced by a brokerage commission and other costs, which can produce a small loss.

> ▪ The IRS does not require Form 1099-B in some cases where you sell shares the same day you exercise the option, but you still have to report the sale on your tax return.

Can My IRA Exercise My Option?

You pay taxes, your IRA doesn't. That simple fact may lead you to the idea of having your IRA exercise your options. If it worked, you would get the benefit of the economic bargain inherent in your options, while the tax consequences would be deferred until you draw money from your IRA.

Unfortunately, options and IRAs don't mix. Regardless of whether you have nonqualified options or ISOs, you can't use your IRA to exercise options you received as compensation. This planning idea violates IRA rules and provides no tax benefits. Even if your company permits you to do this, and you slip it by your IRA provider, you won't be happy with the results.

To see what the problem is, ask yourself who exercised the option. There are only two candidates: you, or the IRA. Either answer has bad consequences.

You exercised. If you exercised the option (rather than the IRA), then you failed to shift the tax consequences of exercising from yourself to the IRA. You have to report income equal to the bargain element if you exercised a nonqualified option. The same is true if you exercised an incentive stock option, because your exercise is followed immediately by a disqualifying disposition of the stock. So you didn't accomplish anything positive.

At the same time you have a big negative. You aren't permitted to transfer property other than cash to an IRA, except in connection with a rollover from a qualified retirement plan or another IRA. Option plans are *not* qualified retirement plans. Violating this rule can result in severe penalties. End result: without accomplishing anything positive, you've created an expensive mess by violating the rule against contributing property to an IRA.

Your IRA exercised. But what if your IRA itself exercises the option? The answer is just as bad. The only way the IRA can exercise the option is if you have transferred the option from yourself to the IRA. Without such a transfer, it's you exercising the option, not the IRA. As we've seen, you're not permitted to transfer property other than cash to an IRA. Your option is property, so you've violated that rule if the IRA exercises the option.

You've also failed to shift the tax consequences. By definition, your option is a nonqualified option at this point, because ISOs are not transferable. The IRS has ruled that if a nonqualified option is transferred to another person, a subsequent exercise of the option results in compensation income to the original owner. Even if you could somehow get around the rule against transferring property to an IRA, you haven't avoided the need to report income upon exercise of the option.

In short. If this idea occurred to you as a way to handle your options, give yourself credit for creativity—and then move on to other ideas. Any way you look at it, this idea is a loser.

Part IV
Nonqualified Stock Options

Nonqualified stock options are one of the most popular forms of equity compensation. Companies like them because they provide a flexible and efficient way to attract, retain and motivate employees (and other service providers, such as directors and consultants). Workers like them because they represent an opportunity to grow wealth, with tax consequences deferred until the year of exercise.

This part of the book assumes you're familiar with the material in Part III.

Part IV
Nonqualified Stock Options

Chapter 14
Exercising Nonqualified Stock Options

Your nonqualified stock option gives you the right to buy stock at a specified price. You exercise that right when you notify the company of your purchase in accordance with the terms of the option agreement. The tax consequences of exercising a nonqualified stock option depend on whether the stock is vested when you receive it and the manner of exercising the option.

Normal Exercise

The normal way to exercise a nonqualified stock option is to pay the purchase price in cash. When you do this, your tax consequences are the same as for a non-option purchase of stock from your company. Chapter 8 describes those ruled in detail. Briefly, there are three possible treatments:

Stock is vested. You receive the stock with no strings attached (or the strings aren't enough to keep the stock from being vested). This is the most common situation. When this happens you report compensation income equal to the *bargain element* in your option: the difference between the fair market value of the stock on the day you exercised the option and the amount you paid for the stock. You have to report this income regardless of whether you sell the stock. If you're an employee, the company has to withhold income tax on this amount, and that usually means you have to come up with cash for the withholding in addition to the purchase price.

Example: Your option permits you to buy 1,000 shares at $25 per share. When you exercise, the stock is trading at $32. You'll report $7,000 of income (1,000 shares times the $7 spread per share). To exercise, you had to pay the $25,000 exercise price plus about $2,200 to cover withholding on the $7,000 of income.

Stock is not vested. Some companies require you to earn the right to keep the stock after you exercise the option. If there's a period of time when you can't keep the stock—or at least get full value for it—if you stop working for the company, your stock isn't vested. In this case, unless you file the *section 83b election* (see below), you report no income when you exercise the option. Instead, you report income when the stock vests. The amount of income is the difference between the fair market value of the stock *on the vesting date* and the amount you paid for it.

Example: Same as the previous example, except this time the option agreement says you have to sell the stock back at the $25 purchase price if your employment ends within the next year. You don't file the section 83b election. That means you don't report income when you exercise the option. A year later, when the stock vests, the value is $38 per share. At that time you report $13,000 of compensation income (1,000 shares times the difference between the $38 value and your purchase price of $25). Your company may require you to make a payment to cover withholding before releasing the shares to you.

Section 83b election. If your stock isn't vested when you receive it, you can choose to treat it as if it were vested. You do this by filing a "section 83b election" *within 30 days after you exercise the option.* If you file this election, you avoid having to report a larger amount of compensation income if the value of the stock goes up during the vesting period. Your tax treatment will be the same as in the first example above.

These rules are spelled out in more detail in Chapter 8.

Basis and Holding Period

It's important to keep track of your basis in stock. Basis determines how much gain or loss you report when you sell the stock. When you exercise a nonqualified option your basis is equal to the amount you paid for the stock *plus* the amount of income you report for exercising the option.

> **Example:** You bought stock worth $40 per share for $15 per share, reporting $25 per share of compensation income. Your basis is $40 per share: the $15 per share you paid to exercise the option plus the $25 per share you reported as compensation income. If you sell the stock later for $45 per share, your gain will be only $5 per share, even though you paid just $15 per share for the stock. The $5 per share profit will be capital gain, not compensation income.

For certain limited purposes (particularly under Section 16b of the Securities Exchange Act of 1934) you're treated as if you owned the stock during the period you held the option. This rule doesn't apply when you're determining what category of gain or loss you have when you sell the stock, though. You have to start from the date you bought the stock by exercising the option, and hold for more than a year to get long-term capital gain.

Cashless Exercise

Some companies make it easy for you to sell some or all of your stock at the same time you exercise the option. The sale proceeds cover your exercise price and withholding obligation, so this is sometimes called a *cashless exercise*. It may seem as if you had just a single transaction because everything happened at once, but when you exercise your options this way you have to report *two* transactions: exercise of the option (as described in this chapter) and sale of the stock (as described in the following chapter). See Chapter 13 for more discussion of cashless exercise.

Using Stock to Exercise an Option

Another way to exercise an option is to use stock you already own to pay the purchase price. Not all companies permit this method of exercise. The special tax considerations for this method of exercising options are explained in Part VI of this book.

Chapter 15
Selling NQO Stock

The tax rules for selling stock you receive from exercising a nonqualified stock option are relatively simple. With this type of option, you reported compensation income at the time of exercise or when the stock vested, so a sale produces capital gain or loss. You merely have to determine your holding period and basis, then report the sale as explained in Chapter 53.

Holding period. Your holding period for tax purposes begins when you exercise the option. You can't include the time you held the option. To get a long-term capital gain, you have to hold the stock at least a year and a day. If you sell earlier than that, any gain or loss will be short-term.

Basis. This is where you have to pay attention. Stock you buy through a broker has a basis equal to the amount you paid to acquire it (including brokerage commissions). Stock you buy when you exercise a nonqualified stock option has a basis equal to the amount you paid *plus the amount of income you reported when you exercised the option.*

Example: You exercised an option to buy stock for $20 per share when the stock was worth $35 per share. You reported compensation income equal to $15 per share. Two years later, you sold the stock at $45 per share.

When you report this sale on your tax return, you show a cost basis of $35 per share: the $20 per share you paid, plus the $15 per share of compensation income you reported. *If you forget to include the compensation income in your basis, you'll pay tax on that amount twice.*

Cashless Exercise

Some companies provide arrangements under which you can exercise your option and sell some or all of the stock at the same time. That way you don't have to come up with any cash at the time you exercise the option. This kind of *cashless exercise* is treated the same as two separate transactions: exercise of the option, followed by sale of the stock. For more on this subject see Chapter 13.

Stock Used to Exercise Option

Some companies permit you to use stock you already own to pay the purchase price when you exercise an option. Part VI of this book explains the special rules that apply in this situation.

Chapter 16
Gifts of Nonqualified Options

Many nonqualified stock option plans do not permit transfers of any kind. In recent years, some companies have made their nonqualified options transferable to a limited extent, usually only for estate planning purposes. You may be able to transfer your shares to family members, trusts, or a family partnership.

> - The terms of your stock option agreement, or terms of the stock option plan under which it was issued, determine whether the option is transferable.

No Income Shift

Such a transfer doesn't shift the income tax consequences of exercising the option. Even though you'll no longer own the option, you'll have to report income when the option is exercised, just as if you were the one to exercise it. The ability to transfer your option is not an opportunity for income tax planning.

Gift and Estate Tax

The benefit from transferring an option comes in connection with gift and estate tax. The option may be an asset that's likely to grow in value very quickly. That's precisely the kind of asset you want to get out of your estate if you're concerned about estate taxes. If you can move the option to an appropriate person or entity before it becomes extremely valuable you may save yourself some estate planning headaches later.

The IRS is aware of this opportunity. They haven't said there's anything wrong with doing this, but they laid out some ground rules in a pair of 1998 rulings that make it more difficult to shift valuable options without claiming much value.

Timing rule. You may receive a nonqualified option that doesn't permit immediate exercise. For example, the option may permit you to buy 300 shares at a specified price, but provide that you have to continue to work for the company one year to exercise the first 100, another year for the next 100 and yet another year before you can exercise the entire option.

The IRS has ruled that in this circumstance, you have not made a completed gift of the option until it becomes exercisable. The reasoning is that the option doesn't have any value unless you continue to work for the company. It isn't until you complete this service requirement that we can definitely say you transferred something of value.

This ruling is *bad news* for those who want to make an early transfer of nonqualified stock options. If you value the gift at the time of the transfer, it might be possible to argue that a discount applies because the donor has to keep working. By delaying the effective date of the gift, the IRS eliminates this possible discount. What's more important, if the company's stock rises in value during the period it takes for the option to become exercisable, the value of the option—and the potential gift tax liability—can increase dramatically. Depending on circumstances, a small percentage increase in the value of the stock can cause a large percentage increase in the value of the option.

If you're considering a gift of a nonqualified stock option, you should carefully consider the effect of this ruling. The ruling does not prohibit gifts prior to vesting, but such gifts become something of a gamble if an increase in the stock price can be anticipated. You don't know how large the gift is—and therefore the size of the gift tax implications—until after you've made the gift. To avoid unpredictable results, it may be prudent to wait until the options have vested before making a gift.

If the option vests in stages, the ruling states that the gift occurs in stages. It may be possible to handle this by giving only the vested portion of an option and retaining the part that isn't vested. The terms of the option agreement or the plan under which it was issued should tell you whether such a partial transfer is permitted.

Determining value. A companion ruling to the one described above provides a "safe harbor" for valuing certain compensatory stock options for gift tax purposes. This procedure applies only to options with respect to stock of public companies that are subject to FAS 123, an accounting rule that requires disclosure of certain information concerning compensatory options. The revenue procedure calls for the use of certain factors and methodologies used in FAS 123 reporting.

This procedure isn't mandatory. If you use a different valuation methodology you aren't necessarily wrong. But if you use the methodology in the ruling, you can be assured the IRS won't challenge it.

The ruling doesn't provide actual formulas for valuation. It calls for the use of standard valuation methods such as the Black-Scholes model, but the model must be adapted to the terms of the option and take into account anticipated dividends. If you work for a company that's already hiring experts to value its options to comply with FAS 123, it's possible the same experts will provide the service of valuing options for gift tax purposes in accordance with the IRS rules. See Chapter 40 for a discussion of option valuation.

Not Available for ISOs

You can't transfer an incentive stock option other than at death. This is a specific requirement of the Internal Revenue Code. If your option is transferable, it isn't an incentive stock option.

Don't Do This at Home

Estate planning is a very technical area. I have over twenty years of experience as a lawyer, and I wouldn't dream of doing my own estate planning without consulting an expert. Lawyers aren't cheap, but the cost of estate planning expertise is a bargain compared to the cost of making a mistake in this area. That's especially true if you're dealing with complicated assets like equity compensation. When it comes to estate planning, get the kind of help that's appropriate to your level of wealth.

Part V
Incentive Stock Options

Incentive stock options (ISOs) are a form of equity compensation that provides unique tax benefits—and significant tax complexity. This part of the book assumes you're familiar with the option fundamentals explained in Part III.

Part V
Incentive Stock Options

Chapter 17
Overview of
Incentive Stock Options

Incentive stock options may appear to be very similar to nonqualified stock options. In fact, depending on the terms of your options, you may be able to lay a nonqualified option and an ISO side by side and see no difference at all, other than the fact that one is called an incentive stock option and the other is not. Yet ISOs are far more complex. Proper handling of them requires more knowledge, and more detailed planning, than are required for nonqualified options.

There's a reason to endure these headaches, though. Incentive stock options provide the possibility of paying significantly less tax than if you received nonqualifying options. If you can take advantage of this opportunity, you may benefit much more from an ISO than you would from a nonqualified option.

Alternative Minimum Tax

The biggest reason for the complexity of incentive stock options is the alternative minimum tax (AMT). This tax is so complicated that I devote a separate part of the book to explaining how it works. You can expect to pay AMT in the year you exercise an ISO unless you sell the ISO stock the same year. Some or all of the AMT may be allowed in a later year as a credit to reduce your regular income tax, however. You may find that you need professional help in forecasting the true cost of the AMT, and planning to minimize that cost.

Special Holding Period

Another source of complexity is the special holding period that applies to stock you acquire when you exercise an incentive stock option. Your tax consequences are different—and more favorable—if you hold the stock until the *later* of (a) one year after the date you exercised the option, or (b) two years after the date you received the option. Once you reach that point you can sell the stock without reporting any compensation income. All of your profit will be taxed at favorable capital gains rates. There are certain constraints on what you can do with the stock prior to satisfying this requirement. If you're considering disposing of the stock before that time period is up, you need to understand the consequences of an early disposition of ISO stock. Usually you'll have to report compensation income at that time.

> ▪ In our planning section, Chapters 43 and 44 focus on incentive stock options.

Chapter 18
Exercising Incentive Stock Options

The most important difference between incentive stock options and nonqualified options is that you don't have to report compensation income when you exercise an ISO unless you sell the stock at the same time. If you hold your ISO stock long enough, you can avoid reporting compensation income altogether, so all your profit is taxed at favorable capital gain rates. But the tax law also taketh away. You may have to pay a significant amount of tax when you exercise your ISO because of the alternative minimum tax (AMT).

This chapter explains general rules that apply when you exercise incentive stock options. Be sure to consult the appropriate chapters in other parts of this book if you option plan has special features:

- The opportunity to use stock you already own to pay the exercise price for your option (Part VI).

- The opportunity for "early exercise," where you buy stock before it's vested (Chapter 34).

Regular Tax Treatment

For purposes of the regular income tax, the exercise of an incentive stock option is a non-event. Unless you sell the stock at the same time, exercising the option doesn't affect the amount of regular income tax you report in any way.

> • As explained in Chapter 14, you have to report compensation income when you exercise a nonqualified option.

Because you don't report any income when you exercise an incentive stock option, your basis for the stock you acquired is simply the amount you paid for it. Your holding period begins when you acquire the stock. You can't include the period for which you held the option.

No employment tax. For a while there was some question about whether you have to pay employment tax on exercise of incentive stock options. The IRS has thrown in the towel on this issue, so it is now clear there will be no employment tax on this income, even if you sell the shares the same day you exercise the option.

Alternative Minimum Tax

So much for the good news. The bad news is that the exercise of an incentive stock option gives rise to an "adjustment" under the AMT. The adjustment is precisely the amount you would have reported as compensation income if you exercised a nonqualified option instead of an ISO. In other words, it's equal to the amount by which the fair market value of the stock exceeds the amount you paid for it—otherwise known as the *spread* or *bargain element.*

> ▪ The AMT adjustment only applies if you hold the ISO stock at the end of the calendar year in which you exercise the option. If you dispose of your ISO stock before then, you don't report an AMT adjustment. See Chapter 19.

The AMT adjustment has three consequences.

AMT liability. First and most obviously, you may have to pay AMT in the year you exercise an incentive stock option. There's no way to determine the amount of AMT you'll pay simply by looking at the amount of the bargain element when you exercise the option. This adjustment may be the event that triggers AMT liability, but the *amount* of liability depends on many other aspects of your individual income tax return. You may find that you can exercise some ISOs without paying any AMT at all. If your bargain element is large, though, you should expect to pay as much as 28% or more of the bargain element as AMT. The maximum rate for the AMT is 28%, and for large dollar amounts you can use that percentage as a reasonable guesstimate of your AMT liability. The tax resulting from a single item can be greater than that percentage, though—perhaps closer to 35%—because of the way various features of the alternative minimum tax interact.

> ▪ AMT is included when you determine how much estimated tax you have to pay. See Chapter 49.

AMT credit. The second consequence from the AMT adjustment is that some or all of your AMT liability will be eligible for use as a credit in future years. This credit can only be used in years when you *don't* pay AMT. It reduces your regular tax, not your AMT. It's called the AMT credit because it's a credit for having paid AMT in the past.

In the best case, the AMT credit will eventually permit you to recover all of the AMT you paid in the year you exercised your incentive stock option. When that happens, the only effect of the AMT was to make you pay tax *sooner*, not to make you pay *more* tax than you would have paid. But for various reasons you can't count on being able to recover all of the AMT in later years, especially when large dollar amounts are involved.

AMT basis. The third consequence from the AMT adjustment is very important—and easy to overlook. We noted earlier that the stock you acquire when you exercise an ISO has a basis equal to the amount you paid. But the stock has a different basis for purposes of the alternative minimum tax. The stock's AMT basis is equal to the amount you paid *plus* the amount of the AMT adjustment. That means you'll report a smaller amount of gain for AMT purposes when you sell the stock.

Example: You exercise an ISO, paying $35 per share when the value is $62 per share. You report an AMT adjustment of $27 per share. Later, after satisfying the holding period for ISO stock, you sell the stock for $80 per share. For purposes of the regular income tax you report gain of $45 per share ($80 minus $35). But for AMT purposes you report gain of only $18 per share. Your AMT basis is equal to the $35 you paid plus the $27 adjustment you reported.

The difference in the amount of gain results in a *favorable adjustment* for purposes of the AMT. This adjustment can be used to cancel out a positive adjustment you have from exercising more ISOs in the year you sell this stock, perhaps enabling you to exercise ISOs without incurring more AMT liability. If you don't exercise more options in the year you sell your ISO stock, the favorable adjustment will help you use your AMT credit. For further explanation, see Part VII.

> ■ If you overlook the higher AMT basis of your ISO stock when you sell it, you may end up unnecessarily paying double tax with respect to your ISO.

State Taxes

Some states (notably California, home of many companies that provide incentive stock options) have their own version of the alternative minimum tax. When you figure the cost of exercising your ISOs, don't forget the possibility of paying state AMT.

There's potential for a double whammy here. State income tax (including state AMT) is a deduction on your federal return if you itemize. But the deduction isn't allowed when you calculate your federal AMT. Paying state AMT can increase your federal AMT!

Chapter 19
Early Disposition of ISO Stock

Incentive stock options provide a unique benefit: the ability to avoid reporting any of your profit as compensation income. If you wait long enough before selling your stock, all your profit will be long-term capital gain. This chapter is about situations where you *don't* wait long enough.

> ▪ **Tax lingo:** If you sell or otherwise dispose of your ISO stock before the end of the special holding period described below, you've made a *disqualifying disposition*. We use the term *early disposition* to mean the same thing.

Special Holding Period

To avoid an early disposition you have to hold the stock you acquired by exercising your ISO beyond the *later* of the following two dates:

- One year after the date you exercised the ISO, or

- Two years after the date the company granted the ISO to you.

Many employers don't permit exercise of an ISO within the first year after the employee receives it. If that's the case you don't have to worry about holding more than two years after the date your employer granted the option. You'll automatically satisfy that test if you hold more than a year after the date you exercise the option. If you can exercise in the first year, though, and you choose to do so, you'll have the possibility of a disqualifying disposition even after you've held the stock more than a year.

> **Example:** You receive an incentive stock option and exercise it six months later. If you sell the stock thirteen months after exercise, you'll have an early (or disqualifying) disposition even though you held the stock more than a year. The reason: your sale occurred less than two years after you received the option.

What Is a Disposition?

Everyone understands that a *sale* of ISO stock within the special holding period results in a disqualifying disposition. Other types of transfers may or may not be considered dispositions for this purpose.

Death of shareholder. A transfer that occurs as a result of your death is not a disposition for purposes of this rule. Your death during the special holding period will not trigger compensation income.

Transfer to spouse. A transfer of the stock to your spouse—or to a former spouse in connection with a divorce—is not a disqualifying disposition. Following such a transfer, the spouse receiving the stock is subject to the same rules as the one who transferred the stock. If you receive ISO shares from your spouse you should also obtain essential information for tax reporting:

- The date when the special holding period ends.

- The cost basis of the shares.

- The value of the shares on the date the option was exercised.

Gifts. Transfers at death and gifts to your spouse are covered by the rules described above. All other gifts are dispositions. You'll have to report compensation income if you give your ISO stock to an individual or to a charity before the end of the special holding period.

Trusts. A custodial account under the Uniform Transfers to Minors Act (or the Uniform Gifts to Minors Act) is *not* a trust. Transfers to such accounts are gifts, and count as dispositions.

A transfer of ISO stock to a *revocable* trust should not be treated as a disposition. You can terminate this kind of trust and take the stock and other property back whenever you want. For that reason, the tax law treats you as if you still own the stock after you transfer it to a revocable trust.

You've made a disposition, though, if you transfer the stock to an *irrevocable* trust. This type of trust doesn't let you take the stock back out. Generally you'll want to avoid making such a transfer during the special holding period, because it means having to report compensation income.

Transfer to broker. Transferring stock certificates to a broker who will hold the stock in street name isn't a disposition. Any transfer of the shares from the brokerage account will be treated as a transfer by you.

Short sales. The IRS takes the position that a short sale of your company's stock while you hold ISO stock is a disposition, even if the constructive sale rules don't apply.*

Example: You exercised an ISO in March, buying 1,000 shares. In June, you sold short 1,000 shares, while continuing to hold your ISO shares. In September you closed the short sale by purchasing shares in the stock market. You never sold the ISO shares, and the constructive sale rules don't apply. Yet the IRS position is that you made a disqualifying disposition in June when you made the short sale.

Market options. Within limits, you can use options you buy in the stock market to protect your gains in ISO stock without causing a disqualifying disposition. For

---

* Details of the constructive sale rule appear in my book *Capital Gains, Minimal Taxes.*

example, you may be able to buy a put option that protects you against a decline in the value of the stock. Some of the tax consequences of doing this are unclear, however. See Chapter 52 for more on this subject.

Borrowing. Using the stock as collateral for a loan is *not* a disposition. For example, you can hold the stock in a margin account with your broker without triggering compensation income. Of course, you'll have a disposition if the stock is sold to meet your margin requirements, or is otherwise seized as collateral. See below for bankruptcy, however.

Bankruptcy. A special rule protects you from having a disqualifying disposition in bankruptcy. You don't have a disposition when the stock is transferred to a bankruptcy trustee, or when the trustee transfers it to a creditor in satisfaction of a liability.

Regular Tax and Disqualifying Dispositions

The tax consequences of an early disposition apply in the year the disposition occurs. You aren't supposed to go back and amend the return for the year you exercised the option, if that was an earlier year.

Sale to an unrelated person. If your disqualifying disposition is a sale of shares to an unrelated person with no repurchase, your tax consequences are as follows:

- For a sale below the amount you paid for the shares, you don't report any compensation income. Your loss on this sale is reported as a capital loss.

- For a sale above the amount you paid for the shares but no higher than the value of the shares as of the date you exercised the option, report your gain on the sale as compensation income (not capital gain). You need to report the sale on Schedule D (used to report capital gains and losses), but your basis should be equal to the selling price, so that you have no gain or loss on the sale.

- If you sell your shares at a price that's higher than the value of the shares as of the date you exercised the option, you report two different items. The bargain element when you exercised the option (the difference between the value of the shares as of that date and the amount you paid) is reported as compensation income. Any additional gain is reported as capital gain (which is normally short-term).

Other dispositions. There's an unfavorable rule that applies to a disqualifying disposition if it occurs in certain types of transactions. The rule applies in any situation where the tax rules would prevent you from deducting a loss. It doesn't matter if you have an *actual* loss. Even if you have a gain, the rule applies if the disposition was one of the *types* of transactions where losses are not allowed. The problem transactions are (1) gifts, including charitable gifts, (2) sales to relatives or entities (like trusts or businesses) owned by you or your relatives, and (3) any sale where you purchase replacement shares within 30 days before or after the sale.* In any of these situations, the following rules apply:

- You have to report the full amount of the bargain element from when you exercised the option as compensation income. That's true even if the value of the stock has gone down since the date you exercised the ISO.

- If the transaction requires you to report gain (such as a sale to a related person other than your spouse), any gain that exceeds the amount of compensation income should be reported as

---

* As explained in Chapter 51, the wash sale rule can prevent you from claiming a loss when you buy replacement shares during this period.

capital gain (which may be long-term or short-term depending on how long you held the stock).

Example: You paid $10,000 to buy stock worth $110,000 when you exercised your incentive stock option. In December of the same year, the stock is worth $20,000. If you continue to hold the stock until the end of the year you'll owe AMT based on the $100,000 spread, owing roughly $28,000, even though the stock is now worth less than that amount. A normal sale of the stock before the end of the year would allow you to report only $10,000 of income and pay only about $4,000 of tax.

Instead, you donate the stock to your favorite charity. Because of the unfavorable rule described above, you have to report compensation income equal to the original spread: $100,000. You also get a deduction for your charitable contribution, but that's only $20,000, the current value of the stock. You end up paying *regular* income tax (not AMT) on $80,000. It's possible that your tax actually *increased* as a result of making this contribution.

Compensation but no withholding. Any compensation income you have from an early disposition of ISO stock should appear on your W-2 for that year. Even if it doesn't, you should report this income on the same line of your tax return where you report your other wages. (The IRS won't object to seeing a larger number on that line than the amount shown on your W-2.) Although this income is considered compensation, it isn't subject to withholding or employment tax.

AMT Consequences

The alternative minimum tax consequences of an early disposition depend on whether it occurs in the same year you exercise your option.

Disposition in year of exercise. When your disposition occurs in the same year you exercised the option, you have nothing to report for AMT purposes. You don't report anything for exercising the option, and you don't report anything for disposing of the stock, because the two actions cancel each other out under the alternative minimum tax.

Disposition in a later year. When you make an early disposition, but not in the same year you exercised the option, your situation is a little more complicated. The AMT adjustment you reported in the year you exercised the option will give you a negative AMT adjustment (an adjustment in your favor) in the year of the disposition. That adjustment should make it easier for you to claim a credit for the AMT you paid in the year of exercise. See Part VII for more information.

Chapter 20
Sale of Mature ISO Stock

Once you satisfy the special holding period for stock acquired with an incentive stock option, you have *mature ISO stock*. A sale or other disposition of this stock isn't a disqualifying disposition. Any profit you have from a sale will be capital gain, *not* compensation income. In addition, the AMT credit may shield some or all of this gain from tax.

Regular Tax Consequences

For purposes of the regular tax, selling mature ISO stock is just like selling stock you bought on the open market. Your basis is equal to the amount you paid for the stock, and your holding period began when you exercised the option. For more information on reporting sales of stock, see Chapter 53.

AMT Consequences

It's *extremely important* to understand, and properly report, the alternative minimum tax consequences of selling mature ISO stock. A mistake here can cost you a lot of money.

When you exercised your ISO you had to report an *AMT adjustment* that may have required you to pay alternative minimum tax. Regardless of whether the adjustment resulted in a need to pay AMT, the adjustment caused you to have a *dual basis* in your ISO stock. For purposes of the regular income tax your basis is simply the amount you paid to buy the stock. But when it comes to the AMT, you increase your basis by the amount of the AMT adjustment.

The upshot is that you'll report a *negative* AMT adjustment—an adjustment in your favor—when you sell your ISO stock. On the most recent version of Form 6251 (the form used to report your AMT calculation), the adjustment appears on line 9 and should be entered as a negative number. This adjustment can reduce your taxes.

- If you're otherwise subject to AMT liability in the year you sold the ISO stock (perhaps because you exercised a new ISO), the negative adjustment will reduce or eliminate the AMT you pay in the current year.

- If you aren't subject to AMT liability in the year you sold the ISO stock, the negative adjustment increases the gap between your regular tax and the tax that's calculated under the AMT rules. The result may be a larger *AMT credit* in the year you sell the ISO stock.

Part VII of this book provides more information on the alternative minimum tax. In particular, see Chapter 29 concerning dual basis and Chapter 30 for more about the AMT credit.

Part VI
Using Stock to Exercise Options

Some companies allow you to pay the exercise price for an option by turning in shares of stock you already own. This opportunity isn't available under all stock option plans, so check first before you try to do this. If your company allows this form of exercise, read the chapters in this part that apply to your situation.

Part VI
Using Stock to Exercise Options

Chapter 21
Using Stock to Exercise Options

Some companies permit option holders to use shares of stock they already own to pay the purchase price when they exercise an option to buy new shares.

> **Example:** You have an option to buy 600 shares of stock for $5 per share. The current value of the stock is $12 per share. To exercise the option you can pay $3,000 in cash—or, if your company permits, you can "pay" $3,000 in stock. You would turn in 250 shares (250 times the current value of $12 equals $3,000) and receive 600 shares (an increase of 350 shares).

This form of exercise is often very convenient because it relieves the option holder of the need to come up with cash to exercise the option. (Cash will still be required to cover withholding and other tax liabilities, however.) The tax results may be favorable when compared to an alternative where you sell stock to come up with the cash to exercise your option.

Availability

Not all companies permit this form of exercise. The company may not like this approach because it puts fewer shares in the hands of option holders compared to a cash exercise. Possibly the company (or its shareholders) believe that a cash exercise shows greater commitment or has greater integrity. Whatever the reason, you can't *assume* this method of exercise is available. Read your option agreement and the stock option plan under which it was issued, and ask the appropriate person at your company if you're still unsure.

Of course this method of exercise isn't available if you don't own stock in the company. In that case you'll need to use cash, at least for your first purchase. After that you may be able to use stock you bought from an earlier exercise of an option to exercise later options. Be sure to understand the tax consequences before adopting this approach.

Certification Instead of Exchange

You might wonder whether it's necessary to have an actual exchange of shares. After all, the shares you receive in the exchange are identical to the shares you surrender. If you're going to turn in 250 shares to receive 600 that are exactly the same, why not just hold onto the 250 shares and receive 350 new shares?

In private letter rulings, the IRS has said you can do exactly that. The rulings describe a process in which you certify that you own the shares that are needed for the exchange. If the shares are held by a registered securities broker in street name on your behalf, you would submit a notarized statement attesting to the number of shares owned. If you hold the certificates yourself, you would submit the certificate numbers, which can be checked against the records of the transfer agent. The IRS says this is good enough to count as constructive delivery of the shares.

If available, this approach can save time and money in situations where it may be costly to actually tender the shares. If you're using the shares as collateral for a loan, for example, you may need the lender's permission to transfer the shares. In any event, the paperwork involved in the certification process is likely to be less cumbersome than tendering the shares.

Tax Consequences

The tax consequences of using stock to exercise an option depend on the type of option. See Chapter 22 for non-qualified options, and Chapters 23 and 24 for incentive stock options.

Chapter 22
Using Stock to Exercise Nonqualified Options

Chapter 21 describes the general idea of using stock to exercise options. This chapter explains the tax consequences when you use stock to exercise a nonqualified option. These consequences are unusual and interesting. You're treated as if two separate things happened:

- You made a *tax-free exchange* of old shares for an equal number of new shares (the "exchange shares"), *and*

- You received *additional* shares (the "added shares") for zero payment.

As to the *exchange* shares you don't report any income. The shares you receive in the exchange have the same basis and holding period as the shares you turned in. It's as if you simply continued to hold the old shares.

As to the *added* shares, you have to report the value as compensation income when you receive them (or when they vest, if later), the same as if you received a grant or award of stock, as explained in Chapter 8. Those shares take a basis equal to the amount of compensation income you report, and your holding period begins when you acquire them (or when they vest).

> **Example:** You have an option to buy 600 shares of stock for $5 per share (a total of $3,000). You exercise the option by turning in 250 shares worth $12 per share. Assuming the shares are vested when you receive them, you would end up with 250 shares that have the same basis and holding

period as the shares you turned in, plus 350 shares with a basis of $12 per share and a holding period that begins when you acquire the shares.

Identification. When you decide to sell some of your shares, it will be important to determine which shares you want to sell. In some cases you'll want to sell the newer shares because they have a higher basis. In other cases you may want to sell the older shares to get long-term gain instead of short-term gain. Be sure you understand the principles and procedures for identifying shares as explained in Chapter 50.

Using ISO shares. It may be possible to use shares you own from a previous exercise of an incentive stock option to pay the purchase price on exercise of a nonqualified stock option. This exchange will not be treated as a disposition of the ISO stock, but the exchange shares will *continue* to be ISO shares. That means a subsequent sale of those shares may cause you to report compensation income if you haven't satisfied the special holding period. In the example above, if you turned in 250 ISO shares, then 250 of the shares you received in the exchange would be treated as ISO shares with the same basis and holding period as the shares you turned in.

> ■ **Caution:** The same rule doesn't apply if you use ISO shares to exercise an ISO. Chapter 23 explains the rules for using stock to exercise an ISO.

Evaluation

This method of exercising an option doesn't produce any magical benefits. The greatest advantage is in situations where you would have to sell stock you already own in order to come up with the money you need to exercise the option. In this case, using stock to exercise the option permits you to avoid reporting gain from a sale of those shares. But you'll report the gain eventually, so this is a tax deferral, not a tax reduction.

If one of the alternatives available to you is combined exercise and sale (or *cashless exercise*), as explained in Chapter 13, you should find that the method described in this chapter has almost exactly the same consequences— provided that you sold only enough of the newly purchased shares to pay the exercise price. Normally, the sale portion of that transaction produces very little gain or loss, and you end up holding the same number of shares (and reporting the same amount of income) as if you had used stock to exercise your option.

Of course, you don't necessarily have to use either of these "cashless" methods to exercise your option. You can use funds you have available from another source— savings, perhaps, or taking out a loan—to exercise the option. Comparing this alternative to a "cashless" exercise is an investment question. Do you want to maximize your holding in the company's stock? If so, use cash from another source to exercise your option. If not, consider a cashless form of exercise, if the company makes it available.

Chapter 23
Using Stock to Exercise ISOs

Chapter 21 describes the general idea of using stock to exercise options. This chapter explains the tax consequences when you use stock to exercise an incentive stock option.

Tax Authorities

The tax consequences described below are based in large part on *proposed regulations* and *private letter rulings*. These authorities aren't binding on the IRS, so it's possible in theory that the IRS could challenge a return filed on the basis of these rules. As a practical matter that's very unlikely because the IRS position on these matters hasn't changed in many years.

Source of the Old Stock

The tax consequences of this form of exercise depend on whether or not you use *immature ISO stock* to exercise the option. You have immature ISO stock if you acquired the stock by exercising an incentive stock option and haven't yet satisfied the special ISO holding period (the later of two years after option grant or one year after exercise). If you're *not* using immature ISO stock to pay for the shares you're buying, the shares you're using can be any of the following:

- *Mature* ISO stock (in other words, stock you acquired by exercising an incentive stock option long enough ago that you've satisfied the special ISO holding period).

- Stock from exercising nonqualified stock options.

- Stock acquired in any other way, including purchases on the open market.

Using Shares Other than Immature ISO Shares

Generally, if you're going to use stock to exercise an ISO, you want to use shares *other than* immature ISO stock. Here are the *regular tax* consequences when you do so:

- For regular tax purposes, you don't report any income on the exercise of the incentive stock option. (This rule is the same as if you used cash to exercise your option.)

- You don't report any gain or loss on the shares you used to pay the purchase price on the option. That's because you've made a tax-free exchange of those shares for ISO shares.

- The shares you receive are divided into two batches. One batch includes a number of shares equal to the number of shares you turned in (the *exchange shares*). The other group includes all the additional shares you received (the *added shares*).

- The exchange shares have the same basis as the shares you turned in. They also have the same holding period as the shares you turned in—but only for purposes of determining whether any capital gain or loss on a sale is long-term. For purposes of determining whether you've satisfied the special ISO holding period, your holding period for these shares begins on the date you exercise the option.

- The added shares have a basis equal to the amount of cash (if any) you paid to exercise the option. This amount may be zero or close to zero because you used stock to pay most or all of the exercise price. These shares have a holding period that begins when you receive them.

- Both the exchange shares and the added shares are subject to the rules that cause you to report compensation income if you make a *disqualifying disposition* before satisfying the special ISO holding period.

There are some quirks in the way the rules for disqualifying dispositions apply after you use stock to exercise an ISO. See Chapter 24 for details.

AMT consequences. The IRS hasn't spelled out the consequences under the alternative minimum tax in as great detail as the regular tax consequences. The following results would be consistent with the approach the IRS has taken in this area:

- When you use stock to exercise an ISO, you have to report an AMT adjustment in the same amount as if you had used cash to exercise the option.

- The exchange shares have the same AMT basis as the shares you used to pay the exercise price.

- The added shares have an AMT basis equal to the amount of cash you paid (if any) *plus* the amount of the AMT adjustment.

The significance of AMT basis is explained in Chapter 29.

Using Immature ISO Shares

Because of a special rule—sometimes called the *anti-pyramid rule*—it's generally undesirable to use immature ISO stock to exercise an incentive stock option. Here are the consequences:

- For regular income tax purposes, you don't report any income on the exercise of the new ISO.

- However, *you've made a disqualifying disposition of the immature ISO stock you turned in.* That means you have to report compensation income equal to the bargain element from the exercise of the *old* ISO (the one you exercised to acquire the immature ISO stock). You can't reduce the amount you report as compensation income even if the stock has declined in value since the date of the previous option exercise.

- At the same time, the disposition of the immature ISO stock is treated in part as a tax-free exchange. So apart from the compensation income you report as described above, you don't report gain or loss on the exchange of old ISO shares for new ISO shares, even if the stock has gone up in value since the previous option exercise.

- The shares you receive are divided into two groups. One group includes a number of shares equal to the number of shares you turned in (the *exchange shares*). The other group includes all the additional shares you received (the *added shares*).

- The exchange shares have the same basis as the shares you turned in, increased by the amount of compensation income reported because of the disqualifying disposition. They also have the same holding period as the shares you turned in—but only for purposes of determining whether any capital gain or loss on a sale is long-term. For purposes of determining whether you've satisfied the special ISO holding period, your holding period for these shares begins on the date you exercise the new ISO.

- The added shares have a basis equal to the amount of cash (if any) paid to exercise the option. This may be zero or close to zero because you used stock to pay most or all of the exercise price. These shares have a holding period that begins on the date you exercised the new ISO.

- Both the exchange shares and the added shares are subject to the rules that require you to report compensation income if you make a disqualifying disposition.

See Chapter 24 for a discussion of early disposition after using stock to exercise an ISO.

AMT consequences. The following description of alternative minimum tax consequences would be consistent with the approach the IRS has taken in this area:

- You have to report an AMT adjustment on the exercise of the new ISO in the same amount as if you had used cash to exercise the option.

- The exchange shares have the same AMT basis as the shares you used to pay the exercise price. (The AMT basis of the shares you used to pay the exercise price already included the bargain element from exercise of the original ISO.)

- The added shares have an AMT basis equal to the amount of cash you paid (if any) *plus* the amount of the AMT adjustment.

The significance of AMT basis is explained in Chapter 29.

Chapter 24
Early Disposition After Stock Exercise

Chapter 23 describes the tax consequences of using stock to exercise an incentive stock option. Yet it doesn't describe the tax consequences of an early disposition of shares after using stock to exercise an ISO. As it turns out, this is a tricky little puzzle, and certain interpretations of the rule here could work in your favor—or against you.

> ▪ **Steep climbing.** This chapter contains expert analysis that many readers will find difficult.

Overview

It's easier to see the issues if we have a set of facts in front of us:

Example: You have an ISO that lets you buy 100 shares at $10 per share (total exercise price of $1,000). The stock is currently trading at $25. You already own 40 shares you bought on the open market at $5. At the current price of $25 per share, the 40 shares you already own are worth $1,000, the exercise price of the option. So you use these shares to exercise the option, surrendering 40 shares as "payment" and getting back 100 shares.

Here are some of the questions you have to deal with if you make a disqualifying disposition:

- What shares do you sell first if you sell only some of the shares? Will the sale come first from the exchange shares, or first from the added shares? Or will it be a pro rata portion of both? Can you use share identification (Chapter 50) to choose which shares you sell first?

- How much compensation income do you have to report when you sell some or all of the exchange shares? Or when you sell some or all of the added shares?

The IRS has never provided official guidance that would answer these questions. Proposed regulations issued many years ago provided partial answers, but proposed regulations are just what their name indicates: a proposal, not official guidance that is binding on taxpayers or the IRS. More recently (June 2003) the IRS issued new proposed regulations for incentive stock options, but still made a mess of these issues. So we still have no official guidance, and the unofficial guidance of the proposed regulations isn't very good.

Shares Sold First

The proposed regulations say that if you sell some of the shares, but not all of them, you are deemed to have sold the shares with the lowest basis first. In nearly all cases, that means the added shares are sold first, because those shares have zero basis. The proposed regulations don't tell us which shares are considered sold first if the exchange shares also have zero basis.

The main problem with this rule is that it appears only in a proposed regulation, and we seem to get a different result if we look elsewhere. Generally you're allowed to identify which shares you sell (see Chapter 50), and the authority for doing that appears in a *real* regulation. That means you should be able to sell the exchange shares first if that gives you a better result—at least until the IRS comes out with final regulations dealing with this issue. What's more, if you don't identify shares, the *real* regulations say you sold the oldest shares first, and that seems to mean the exchange shares (which have a holding period that goes back to when you bought the shares you turned in) rather than the added shares. The upshot is that we have a rule in the proposed regulation that seems to conflict with existing rules.

> ■ Some practitioners and employers act as if they have to follow the rule in the proposed regulation, even though it is only a proposal, not a binding legal authority.

Compensation Income

So far, so bad. Now we have to figure out how much compensation income to report when you make a disqualifying disposition. The proposed regulations give some guidance on this issue, but aren't entirely clear. We have to guess what they mean, using some of their examples. Then we have to decide whether we should follow the rules in the proposed regulations, or ignore them because they haven't been adopted as final regulations—or because they appear to be wrong.

The proposed regulations say that when you figure out the amount of compensation income, you should treat the exchange shares as if the amount paid for them was the fair market value on the date of the exchange ($25 in our example). You treat the added shares as if the amount paid for them was zero. This approach is going to give us some strange results.

Suppose you sell 75 of the shares for $30 per share. In our example, the 100 shares you acquired have an overall bargain element of $1,500 because you paid $10 per share when they had a value of $25 per share. It might seem logical that you would have to report compensation income equal to 75% of the bargain element (plus some capital gain) when you sell 75% of the shares, but the proposed regulations say you have to report the entire $1,500 as compensation income. The reason is that the entire bargain element is built into the added shares, and you are deemed to sell those shares first. You don't get any credit for continuing to hold the remaining 25 shares.

It gets worse. Suppose the stock price drops back to $10 before you get around to selling any shares, and then you sell 75 shares at this price. You didn't make any profit at all on your option because you sold at a price equal to your original exercise price. Yet it appears you would have to report compensation income under the proposed regulations. These shares had a fair market value of $1,875 when you exercised the option ($25 per share). The amount paid for the shares was just $375, because the proposed regulations treat you as if you paid zero for the 60 added shares and $25 per share for the 15 exchange shares. The difference is $1,500, but you don't have to report the entire amount as compensation income because this income is limited to your gain on the sale. Your gain on the sale is $675 because you sold 60 shares with zero basis and 15 shares with basis of $5 per share (the original cost of the exchange shares. Apparently you have to report $675 as compensation income in this situation even though you sold the shares at a price equal to the exercise price of the stock option and therefore ended up with zero profit.

A more sensible result. I submitted extensive comments on the proposed regulations, and this was one of the issues I addressed.* The solution I proposed was to determine the amount of compensation income in a disqualifying disposition the same way as if you used cash to pay the exercise price of your stock option. That way you would get credit for continuing to hold 25 shares in the first version of the example above, and you would not report any compensation income at all in the second version where you ended up selling at $10 per share with no profit from your stock option. There's no word yet on whether the IRS will adopt this suggestion in the final regulations.

---

* I submitted these comments on behalf of National Board of Certified Option Advisors Inc. They are available on the web at **www.nbcoa.com**.

Chapter 25
Deferring Income from Nonqualified Options

A provocative question: *Can I exercise my nonqualified options without reporting income?* No one knows for sure whether you can or not. There's a theory that you can, if you're willing to take some risk. The idea here is not to avoid reporting income altogether, but to delay it until a later year.

Words of Caution

The idea for deferring income from nonqualified options has been around for a few years. Some experts in this area believe it works; others aren't so sure. The IRS is aware of this planning technique but so far hasn't taken a position on it. There's no question some people are using it, but that doesn't mean it's completely safe.

In any case, this technique isn't available to everyone. Your company must be willing to set up the appropriate arrangements, and you need to own stock that can be used to exercise your option.

How It Works

The theory for this deferral technique is based on the bifurcated treatment that applies if you use stock to pay the purchase price when you exercise a nonqualified option. As Chapter 22 explains, in this situation you end up with two batches of stock. One batch, which I call the *exchange shares*, is considered to be received in a tax-free exchange for the old shares you used to buy the stock. The other batch, which I call the *added shares*, represent your income from exercising the option.

Now suppose your employer offers you an opportunity to turn in enough old shares to exercise your option without receiving the full number of shares to which you're entitled. Instead of receiving exchange shares and added shares, you'll receive exchange shares and a right to future income. The idea is that you have no income from receiving the exchange shares, because that's a tax-free exchange—and you won't have to report income from the added shares because you don't receive them. Instead, you'll report income when you actually receive the deferred income.

> **Example:** Six months before you actually exercise your nonqualified option, you notify your employer that you want to receive deferred income rather than added shares when you use shares to exercise the option. After waiting six months, you turn in enough shares to exercise the option and receive the same number of shares in return: the *exchange* shares. You don't report any income or gain on the exchange.
>
> In addition, you receive a right to a cash payment at some specified point in the future—say, ten years from now. Until then, the amount of the deferred payment will be adjusted to provide you with some kind of market return, which could be interest at the prime rate or a return based on the performance of a stock index, for example. When the 10 years are up, you receive (and report as compensation income) a cash payment equal to the deferred amount with the investment return.

Notice that you have to notify the employer six months ahead of time if you want to take advantage of this deferral arrangement. No one knows for sure that the six-month period is long enough to make you safe, or that you couldn't use a shorter period. Some experts might suggest that you have to give this notice six months ahead of time *and* in the preceding year. The point of this requirement is to defeat a possible argument of the IRS that you have *constructive receipt* of the income when you exercise the option, because you had a choice at that time (or shortly before that time) to receive current income or deferred income.

Another point: your deferred income is *vested* (you won't lose it if your employment terminates)—but it isn't *secured*. If the company encounters financial difficulties and is unable to pay all its debts, the amount owed to *you* may be one of the debts that goes unpaid.

Evaluation

The tax issues involved in determining whether this technique works are somewhat theoretical. There's some tax risk in using this approach, and credit risk as well. Furthermore, you can't use this approach unless the company is willing to set up the necessary arrangements. There are a variety of good reasons why a company may not want to do so. If the company does want to pursue this approach, it's important to have it structured by an expert familiar with this type of arrangement, to provide the most favorable structure and advise on the risks.

Chapter 26
Reload Options

A twist on options that began appearing in the late 1980's has attracted some popularity—and some controversy. In these arrangements, when you use stock to exercise options, you get new options for each share of stock you surrendered. Your new option may be called a restoration or replacement option. An option that permits you to receive a replacement option is called a *reload option*.

How They Work

If your option has a reload feature, it generally applies only if you use stock to exercise the option. For each share you turn in, you receive a new option priced at the current value of the stock. Usually the new option expires at the same time the old one would have expired.

> **Example:** You hold an option to buy 1,000 shares of your company's stock at $12 per share. The stock is currently trading at $16. You exercise the option, paying the purchase price with 750 shares of stock you already own. You receive 1,000 shares (increasing your total by 250) plus a new option to buy 750 shares at $16 per share.

Without the reload feature, you would simply receive 1,000 shares. That's certainly a benefit: you own 250 more shares than you did before you exercised the option. But the reload feature gives you something more: a new option that allows you to profit from further appreciation in the value of the company's stock.

Other Terms

There's no standard way to provide reload options. If you receive such an option, it's important to read the agreement carefully to understand exactly how it works. Here are some of the possible provisions:

- The reload feature may apply only when you use shares you've owned for a specified period of time, or it may apply only when you use shares you previously acquired under the company's stock option plan.

- You may have to wait a specified period of time before exercising the reload option, or be limited in the number of times you can get reloads. Sometimes the replacement option doesn't include a reload feature, so you only get one bite at the apple.

Tax Consequences

The tax consequences of reload options are no different from the tax consequences of options without this feature. You don't report income of any kind when you receive an option from your company. Receiving a new option when you exercise the old one is certainly a valuable benefit, but it doesn't affect your taxes until you exercise the replacement option.

Strategy

It's difficult to offer strategies for reload options because of variations in the terms. One general point may help guide your strategy, though. When you exercise a normal stock option, you forfeit the remaining time value of the option. That's not true for a reload option. In fact, the time value of the replacement option you receive when you exercise your reload option can be greater than the time value of the option you exercised—even though the new option is for a smaller number of shares.

Example: You have an option to buy 1200 shares at $40 per share. The current value of the stock is $60 per share and the option has three years to run. If you pay cash to exercise the option, you gain access to the built-in $24,000 profit, but you give up more than $16,000 in remaining time value.*

Using the reload feature, you can exercise the option by turning in 800 shares of stock you already own. You can sell the 400 "new" shares, once again gaining access to the built-in $24,000 profit. At the same time you receive an option to buy 800 shares at $60 per share. Even though this option pertains to fewer shares, its time value is actually higher than the time value of option you exercised. You gained access to your $24,000 profit while *increasing* the time value of your option, rather than forfeiting it.

It may seem strange that the new option has a higher time value than the old one. The reason is that time value becomes smaller as the option spread becomes larger. See Chapter 40 for more on option valuation.

Implications. Because you don't sacrifice time value when you exercise a reload option, you should be less reluctant to exercise ahead of the expiration date. Use the reload feature to gain access to profit that has built up in your option to make diversified investments that reduce your risk related to holding a concentrated position in your company's stock. If the new option you get when you exercise is also a reload option, so you can exercise repeatedly, it makes sense to exercise every time your option has acquired substantial value. If your option permits only a single reload, you'll have to be judicious in choosing a time to exercise that permits you to capture substantial value while the option still has time to run.

---

* These numbers assume 5% interest, 60% volatility and no dividends.

Controversy

Reload options are somewhat controversial, with some people saying they are too generous, and don't represent good compensation policy. I wonder whether the critics truly understand the program. In particular, they may be overlooking two points that put reload options in perspective.

The first is that a reload option, although more valuable than an option without this feature, has a *maximum* value equal to the value of the number of shares of stock the initial option permits you to buy. That's true no matter how many times it reloads or how long it extends into the future. It's a mathematical fact that you can't wring more value from a reload option than you would get from owning that number of shares. They don't have potentially infinite value, as some critics seem to suggest.

The other point is that the maximum number of shares the company can end up issuing under all the exercises of a repeating reload option is equal to the number of shares you can buy under the original option. For example, if you start with an option to buy 100 shares, and you exercise by turning in 80 shares, you get 20 new shares and an option for another 80. The company has issued 20 shares, and now has an option outstanding for 80. The total is still 100, and always will be. The potential dilution from a reload option is the same as from an option without this feature.

Reload options may sound like some magical pyramid scheme, but they're not. They provide significant value to the holders, but the cost to the company is limited, just as it is for traditional options.

Part VII
Alternative Minimum Tax (AMT)

The alternative minimum tax affects a small but growing percentage of taxpayers. When it applies, the cost can be substantial. What's worse, this tax is so complicated that it's often difficult to predict when it will apply. Recipients of equity compensation have a particular interest in AMT because of two situations that bring it into play: exercise of incentive stock options, and large long-term capital gains.

There is some good news associated with AMT. In many cases you can recover some or all of your AMT as a credit against your regular tax in a later year. To take full advantage, you have to understand *dual basis* as well as the credit itself.

Part VII
Alternative Minimum Tax

Chapter 27
Overview of AMT

The basic idea behind the alternative minimum tax is a good one: people with very high levels of income shouldn't be able to completely avoid paying income tax while the rest of us pony up each year. The AMT is a poor reflection of that idea, however. Many high-income individuals escape its reach—and every year it ensnares more and more people who were never intended to be affected.

Whatever its merits or demerits, the AMT is a potential problem you have to deal with if you receive equity compensation. It's of particular interest to people who have incentive stock options because exercise of ISOs frequently brings AMT into play. And it isn't just a matter of paying tax when you exercise your ISOs. You also have to understand the consequences when you sell the stock you acquired by exercising the options.

We'll see that the AMT can also apply if you have a large long-term capital gain. That means you can get hit with AMT even if you never had an incentive stock option. If you used nonqualified options to acquire stock that went up in value after you acquired it, for example, you could end up with a large long-term capital gain—and an AMT problem.

Overview

The alternative minimum tax is an extra tax some people have to pay on top of the regular income tax. The original idea behind this tax was to prevent people with very high incomes from using deductions, exclusions and credits to pay little or no tax. For various reasons, though, the AMT reaches more people each year, including some people who don't have lots of special tax benefits. Congress has studied ways to correct this problem, but so far all we've seen is partial, temporary fixes. Until we see comprehensive AMT relief, almost anyone is a potential target for this tax.

The name comes from the way the tax works. The AMT provides an *alternative* set of rules for calculating your income tax. In theory these rules determine a *minimum* amount of tax that someone with your income should be required to pay. If you're already paying at least that much because of the "regular" income tax, you don't have to pay AMT. But if your regular tax falls below this minimum, you have to make up the difference by paying alternative minimum tax.

Q: How do I know if I have to worry about the AMT?

A: Unfortunately, there's no good answer to this common question—which is one of the big problems with the AMT. You can have AMT liability because of one big item on your tax return, or because of a combination of many small items. Some things that can contribute to AMT liability are items that appear on many tax returns, such as a deduction for state income tax or interest on a second mortgage, or even your personal and dependency exemptions. There's a list of such items later in this chapter. If you use computer software to prepare your tax return, the program should be able to do the AMT calculation. If you're preparing a return by hand, the only way to know for sure is to fill out Form 6251—a laborious process.

There are two essential pieces to the AMT. First, you need to understand how your *AMT liability* is calculated for a year when you pay AMT. And second, you need to know how the *AMT credit* can reduce your taxes in years *after* the year you paid alternative minimum tax.

AMT Liability

The best way to understand alternative minimum tax liability is to see how it's calculated. Here's the big picture.

Compute an alternate tax. First, you figure the amount of tax you would owe under a different set of income tax rules. What's different about these rules? Broadly speaking, three things:

- Various tax benefits that are available under the regular income tax are reduced or eliminated.

- You get a special deduction called the *AMT exemption,* which is designed to prevent the AMT from applying to taxpayers with modest income. This deduction *phases out* when your income reaches higher levels, a fact that causes significant problems under the alternative minimum tax.

- You calculate the tax using AMT rates, which start at 26% and move to 28% at higher income levels. By comparison, the regular tax rates start at 10% and then move through a series of steps to a high of 35%.

The result of this calculation is the amount of income tax you would owe under the "alternative" system of tax.

Compare with the regular tax. Then you compare this tax with your regular income tax. If the regular income tax is *higher,* you don't owe any AMT. If the regular income tax is lower than the AMT calculation, though, the difference between the two taxes is the amount of AMT you have to pay.

Example 1: Your regular income tax is $47,000. When you calculate your tax using the AMT rules, you come up with $39,000. That's lower than the regular tax, so you don't pay any AMT.

Example 2: Your regular income tax is $47,000. When you calculate your tax using the AMT rules, you come up with $58,000. You have to pay $11,000 of AMT on top of $47,000 of regular income tax.

If you're paying attention, you've probably noticed that the total amount of tax you pay in Example 2 is equal to the tax calculated under the AMT: $58,000. But it's important to note that you actually pay $47,000 of regular tax plus $11,000 of AMT, as we'll see below.

Reporting and paying the tax. To calculate and report your AMT liability you need to fill out *Form 6251, Alternative Minimum Tax—Individuals.* The instructions for that form are very useful, particularly because the IRS discontinued the publication it used to put out on the AMT.

> • You're required to take your AMT liability into account in determining how much estimated tax you pay. See Chapter 49 on estimated tax.

AMT Credit

Here's good news: a portion of your AMT liability—perhaps all—may reduce the tax you owe on future tax returns. Whether you receive the AMT credit depends in part on the type of items that gave rise to your AMT liability, and in part on your tax calculation for the year in which you claim the credit. See Chapter 30 for details.

Top Ten Things that Cause AMT Liability

Here's a list of items that can cause (or contribute to) liability under the alternative minimum tax. The list isn't *complete*—there are still other items that can contribute to AMT liability. Based on my experience, the items described below are likely to affect more people than the other items. For a complete list, see IRS Form 6251 and the accompanying instructions. By the way, if you count more than 10 items below, just consider it a bonus.

Exemptions. Believe it or not, personal exemptions contribute to AMT liability. The exemptions you claim for yourself, your spouse and your dependents are not allowed when calculating alternative minimum tax. If you have a large number of exemptions, you may run into AMT liability even without taking any of the special tax breaks the AMT was originally aimed at.

> - A taxpayer with a large number of exemptions challenged the AMT in court, saying Congress didn't intend for the tax to apply to someone in his situation. But the law is clear on this point, and the court ruled for the IRS.

Standard deduction. Some 70% of American taxpayers claim the standard deduction (rather than itemizing). The standard deduction isn't allowed under the AMT. Usually this isn't a problem because the AMT generally hits people with higher incomes, and these people are more likely to claim itemized deductions. Yet it's worth noting that a deduction that's so widely used can contribute to AMT liability.

State and local taxes. If you itemize, there's a good chance you claim a deduction for state and local tax, including property tax and state income tax. These deductions are not allowed under the AMT. If you live in a place where state and local taxes are high, you're more likely to pay alternative minimum tax.

Interest on second mortgages. The AMT allows a deduction for interest on mortgage borrowings used to buy, build or improve your principal residence. If you borrowed against your home for some other purpose, the interest deduction may be allowed under the regular income tax but won't be allowed under the alternative minimum tax.

Medical expenses. Yes, medical expenses. The AMT allows a medical expense deduction, but it's more limited than the deduction under the regular income tax. If you claim an itemized deduction for medical expenses, part or all of it will be disallowed when you calculate your alternative minimum tax.

Miscellaneous itemized deductions. Certain itemized deductions are available if your total in this general category is more than 2% of your adjusted gross income. Among the items here are unreimbursed employee expenses, tax preparation fees, and many investment expenses. You can't deduct these items under the AMT, though. If you claim a large number in this area, you could end up paying alternative minimum tax.

Various credits. Many of the credits that are allowed when you calculate your regular income tax aren't allowed when you calculate your AMT. The more credits you claim, the more likely it is that you'll end up paying alternative minimum tax.

- Congress has repeatedly passed temporary laws designed to prevent "personal credits" (such as the child credit, education credits and dependent care credit) from causing AMT liability. As of this writing we are still waiting for Congress to protect these credits from AMT for years after 2003.

Incentive stock options. As detailed in Part V of this book, you have to report an AMT adjustment when you exercise an incentive stock option. Exercising a large ISO is almost certain to cause you to pay alternative minimum tax.

Long-term capital gains. Long-term capital gains receive the same preferential rate under the AMT as they do under the regular income tax. In theory, they shouldn't cause you to pay alternative minimum tax. In practice, it's possible to be stuck with AMT liability because of a large capital gain, as explained in Chapter 28.

Tax-exempt interest. Interest that's exempt from the regular income tax may or may not be exempt from the AMT. It depends on complicated rules that are fully understood only by bond lawyers. Bonds that aren't exempt from AMT pay a slightly higher rate of interest to compensate for the fact that they aren't fully tax-exempt. If you invest in bonds that aren't exempt under the alternative minimum tax, you're a candidate for AMT liability.

Many mutual funds that provide exempt interest invest at least *some* of their money in bonds that aren't exempt under the AMT, to get a higher rate of interest. Their annual statement tells you how much of your income is taxable under the alternative minimum tax.

Tax shelters. The Tax Reform Act of 1986 severely curtailed the ability of most people to reduce their income tax through tax shelters. Yet there are still some legitimate ways of reducing tax liabilities through investments in certain types of partnership arrangements involving such activities as oil and gas drilling. The AMT provides reduced tax benefits for these activities. Always explore alternative minimum tax consequences (among other things) before investing in a tax shelter.

Effective AMT Rate

The effective rate of tax for the AMT (the added tax you actually pay per dollar of added income) can be as much as seven percentage points higher than the nominal rate. That's because the AMT exemption amount gets phased out at the rate of 25% for income above $150,000. If you're in this range of income, adding $100 to your income can added $125 to the amount that is taxed under the AMT because of this phase-out. At the 28% nominal AMT rate the tax on $125 would be $35, so your effective rate for the $100 of added income is 35%—the same as the highest rate under the regular income tax.

Chapter 28
AMT and Long-Term Capital Gain

Congress didn't intend for the alternative minimum tax to apply merely because you have a long-term capital gain. When Congress reduced the capital gain rates in 1997, it provided that the lower rates would apply under the AMT, too. But the way it works out, you may still pay AMT because of a large long-term capital gain.

The AMT Exemption

A major reason for paying AMT in the year of a large capital gain is the *AMT exemption*. This is a special deduction that's designed to prevent the tax from applying at lower income levels. The problem is that the AMT exemption is *phased out* when your income goes above a certain level. Capital gain is income, so it can reduce or eliminate your AMT exemption.

For example, if you're single and your income under the AMT rules is $112,500 or less, you're allowed an AMT exemption of $40,250.* Normally that's enough to prevent you from paying AMT unless you're able to claim special tax benefits that reduce your regular tax. But suppose your income is around that level before you add a $200,000 capital gain (which could come from sale of stock you acquired by exercising an option you received as compensation). Your tax on the capital gain is 15% under both the regular tax and the AMT: $30,000. Under the AMT, though, the added income wiped out your AMT exemption.

---

* This is the exemption amount for years 2003 and 2004. As of this writing, Congress must act to prevent the exemption amount from dropping to a lower level in years after 2004.

How big is the effect? The $40,250 exemption reduces the tax under the AMT calculation by about $11,000. In these facts, the regular tax on this gain is $30,000 and the AMT can be more than $40,000, part of which comes from phasing out the AMT exemption.

That doesn't mean you automatically pay $10,000 of AMT in this situation. Most people have at least a little bit of a cushion between the amount of regular tax they pay and the level where they would have to start paying alternative minimum tax. (The size of your cushion depends on various items, including those listed in the previous chapter.) Besides, the capital gain can cause some tax benefits to phase out under the regular tax, too. But there's a good chance someone in this situation would pay several thousand dollars of AMT.

- During 1998, President Clinton's blind trust sold some assets, causing him to have a large long-term capital gain and incur AMT liability.

Selling ISO Stock

As we'll see in the next chapter, you get an AMT adjustment in your favor when you sell stock acquired by exercising an incentive stock option. Normally this adjustment helps you qualify for the AMT credit. Yet the capital gain effect described in this chapter may work in the opposite direction, making it difficult for you to use the entire credit when you sell your ISO stock.

More Bad News

There's more bad news. People who get caught by the AMT because of a large long-term capital gain usually don't qualify for the AMT credit in later years. The AMT liability is being caused by items that aren't considered *timing* items. Possibly you have some timing items *in addition to* the long-term capital gain, and in that case at least part of your AMT would be available as a credit in later years. More often, this added tax is just a dead loss.

What to Do

In many cases there isn't much you can do about this added tax. But if you're aware of the issue, you may be able to take measures to reduce the impact.

Timing your capital gains. In some situations you can control the year in which you report capital gains. You may be able to delay a sale until after the end of the year, or spread the gain over a number of years by using an installment sale. There's no simple answer to whether these measures help or hurt, so someone has to sharpen a pencil and grind out the numbers.

For example, your gain may be at a level where spreading it over a number of years will keep you out of the AMT—or at least reduce the impact. In this case an installment sale might be an attractive alternative. But suppose your gain is so large that it will phase out your AMT exemption amount many times over. In this situation, you may get a better result by reporting all the gain in one year, so you're only affecting one year's exemption amount.

Timing other items. Another way to plan for the AMT is to see if you can change the timing of other items that are affected by the alternative minimum tax. For example, if you make estimated payments of state income tax, you may try to schedule your payments so they don't fall in the same year as your large capital gain. If that means delaying your state estimates to an extent that causes you to incur a penalty, you'll have to compare the amount of that penalty with the tax savings under the AMT.

Chapter 29
AMT and Dual Basis Assets

Your *basis* in an asset, such as stock or real property, is used to determine how much gain or loss you report when you sell that asset. In some situations an asset may have one basis for regular income tax purposes and a different basis (usually higher) for alternative minimum tax purposes. When that happens, the AMT gain or loss on a sale of that asset won't be the same as the regular tax gain or loss. If you're not alert to this situation you may end up needlessly paying more tax than required.

What Causes Dual Basis

Ordinarily, your basis for an asset is simply the amount you paid for it plus any costs of acquisition (such as brokerage fees). But various events can cause an adjustment in the basis of an asset. For example, if you claim a deduction for depreciation of an asset, you reduce your basis in that asset by the amount of the deduction.

Some of the things that cause an adjustment in basis under the regular tax have a different treatment under the alternative minimum tax. For example, you may have to use a less favorable depreciation schedule for AMT purposes than you use for the regular tax. That means you've claimed smaller depreciation deductions for that asset under the AMT, and as a consequence will have a higher basis in the asset.

Example: Over the years you've used a piece of equipment that cost $20,000, you've claimed depreciation deductions of $12,000, leaving you with an *adjusted basis* of $8,000. During those same years, your AMT depreciation deductions for

the same piece of equipment were only $9,000.
That means your AMT basis is $11,000.

Incentive Stock Options

You have dual basis in stock if you exercise an incentive
stock option and hold the shares until the end of the year.
You have to report an *adjustment* for AMT purposes in
the year of exercise. As a result you may end up paying
alternative minimum tax for that year. But another result
is that your AMT basis in the stock is increased by the
amount of the adjustment.

> **Example:** At a time when your company's stock
> was trading at $80 per share, you exercised an
> incentive stock option to purchase 500 shares at
> $24 per share. For AMT purposes you report an
> adjustment of $28,000 ($56 per share). The result is
> that you hold stock with a basis of $24 per share
> for regular tax purposes and $80 per share for AMT
> purposes.

Sale of Dual Basis Asset

When you sell a dual basis asset, your AMT capital gain or
loss on the sale won't be the same as your regular capital
gain or loss. This can affect your AMT calculation two
ways:

- The difference can reduce your AMT income.

- The difference can affect the part of the AMT
  calculation that applies the 15% rate to AMT long-
  term capital gains.

Typically you'll see an overall reduction in the tax calculated under the AMT as a result of these changes. That
can reduce the amount of AMT you pay in the year you
sold the stock (for example, if you exercised more ISOs
that year), or it can allow you to claim a larger AMT credit
in the year of sale. Yet the difference in basis doesn't
translate *directly* into a reduction in the tax calculated

under the AMT because of the capital loss limitation. As explained below, the AMT adjustment can be smaller—in some cases *much* smaller—than the difference in basis.

AMT Capital Loss Limitation

Under the regular income tax, if you have an overall capital loss (after netting gains against losses), your deduction for that loss is limited to $3,000. Any additional loss carries over to the next year. Under the AMT, the same limitation applies to your *AMT* capital loss, according to the IRS. This limitation can affect the size of the favorable adjustment you claim when you sell stock with dual basis. To find the adjustment amount, you have to compare the amount of capital gain or loss you report on your regular income tax form with the amount you would report using AMT basis for the assets you sold that year. In each case you will take into account all capital gains and losses you had that year (not just the capital gain or loss from the ISO stock) and apply the $3,000 capital loss limitation. The result can be an AMT adjustment in the year of sale much smaller than the adjustment in the year you exercised the option.

> **Example:** In the previous example, you had an AMT adjustment of $28,000 in the year you exercised the option. The stock declined in value by $20,000 between the time you exercised the option and the time you sold the stock in the following year. The sale produced a gain of $8,000 under the regular income tax, but a loss of $20,000 under the AMT due to higher AMT basis. If this is the only item of capital gain or loss on your return for this year, you have an *allowable* AMT capital loss of $3,000. Your favorable AMT adjustment for the sale is $11,000 (the difference between a $3,000 loss and an $8,000 gain). You will enter $11,000 *as a negative number* on line 9 of Form 6251.

	Regular Tax	AMT
Sale of ISO stock	$8,000	($20,000)
Allowed loss		(3,000)
AMT adjustment		(11,000)

You still have another $17,000 of AMT capital loss, but you can't use it this year. This capital loss carries over to the next year, just like a capital loss under the regular income tax.

Other gains and losses. If you have other capital gains and losses in the same year, they have to be included in the calculation on both the regular tax side and the AMT side.

Example: Suppose we change the example above so you have an unrelated capital gain of $2,500. On the sale of ISO stock your regular tax gain was $8,000, so you now have a total of $10,500 in capital gain for purposes of the regular income tax. On the AMT side, you have a loss of $20,000 from the ISO stock and the same unrelated capital gain of $2,500, for an overall loss of $17,500. You're still allowed just $3,000 of that loss in this year, so your allowed loss under the AMT is unchanged. Yet the gain under the regular tax increased by $2,500, so your AMT adjustment increased by $2,500—even though the $2,500 gain was unrelated to the incentive stock option.

	Regular Tax	AMT
Sale of ISO stock	$8,000	($20,000)
Unrelated gain	2,500	2,500
Overall gain (loss)	10,500	(17,500)
Allowed loss		(3,000)
AMT adjustment		(13,500)

The disappearing adjustment. The capital loss limitation can completely eliminate your AMT adjustment, making it difficult to recover your AMT credit.

Example: You paid $50,000 to exercise an incentive stock option on stock worth $150,000. Your choice to hold the stock worked out poorly, and you ended up selling the stock for $30,000 in a year when you had no other capital gains or losses. For regular income tax purposes you have a capital loss of $20,000, and an allowed loss of $3,000. Under the AMT you have a capital loss of $120,000 and an allowed loss of $3,000. Your allowed loss is the same under the regular tax and the AMT, so your AMT adjustment is zero.

	Regular Tax	AMT
Sale of ISO stock	($20,000)	($120,000)
Allowed loss	(3,000)	(3,000)
AMT adjustment		-0-

Why are you saddled with this unhappy result? The idea behind the adjustment is to prevent you from paying a second tax on the same income. You already paid AMT on the $100,000 spread in the year you exercised the option. If you ended up selling the stock for a profit, some or all of the same $100,000 would end up being taxed again under the regular tax. The AMT adjustment is there to prevent that result. But if you have no profit on the sale of the ISO stock—or you pay no tax on that profit because of unrelated capital losses—there is no second tax, and that's why the adjustment is zero in that situation.

AMT Schedule D

To figure the adjustments on Form 6251 (used to report AMT) you should prepare an AMT version of Schedule D (used to report capital gains and losses). You won't file this AMT Schedule D with the IRS, but you need it to fill out Form 6251, which you do file. Keep your AMT Schedule D as part of your tax records for that year.

The AMT Schedule D is the same as your regular Schedule D except it shows a different amount of gain or loss for items with dual basis. All your "normal" gains and losses appear exactly the same on both forms. For sales of ISO stock with dual basis (shares purchased in an earlier year and sold in the current year) the AMT Schedule D will show a smaller gain—or a bigger loss.

You'll compare the AMT Schedule D with the regular Schedule D to determine the size of the favorable adjustment on sale of your ISO stock. You'll also use the numbers from the AMT Schedule D to fill out the part of Form 6251 used to calculate the capital gains rate for AMT purposes.

Chapter 30
AMT Credit

You don't have to be quite so sad (or mad) about paying alternative minimum tax if it reduces the tax you pay in a later year. That's exactly what happens in many cases—but not all. It pays to understand the AMT credit.

Overview

The AMT credit is designed to prevent you from getting stuck paying tax on the same income twice, when the income is taxed under the AMT in one year and taxed under the regular income tax in a later year. The credit is *created* in a year you pay AMT, but *used* in a later year when you *don't* pay AMT. The credit doesn't reduce your AMT. It's called the AMT credit because it arises from paying alternative minimum tax in a prior year.

You need to have a *timing item* to create the AMT credit. A timing item is something that's taxed in one year under the AMT and in a later year under the regular income tax. Incentive stock options can create a timing item because AMT applies in the year of exercise, but the regular income tax doesn't apply until you sell the stock. If you pay AMT because of a capital gain, you don't create a credit because this is not a timing item.

Although you need a timing item to *create* the AMT credit, you don't need a timing item to *use* the credit. You can create the credit by exercising an incentive stock option, and use some or all of the credit in a later year even though you didn't sell any ISO stock that year. Likewise, you don't necessarily get to use the credit in a year you sell the ISO stock, although sale of the stock is often an event that triggers use of most or all of the credit.

> ▪ If you've created an AMT credit by exercising an incentive stock option, you need to file Form 8801 in every subsequent year until the credit is used up.

The Credit as an Asset

A great deal of misunderstanding (and bad tax planning) arises from thinking of the AMT credit as a way to recover tax you paid in the year you had AMT liability. That's true in a sense, but thinking of the credit that way is likely to lead to confusion. Instead, think of it as a way to reduce the tax you pay on income received in later years.

Why is that important? Many people are unhappy with having an unused AMT credit because they think this means the government is holding money they should be able to recover. To "recover" the credit they take steps like selling ISO stock or accelerating other income. They feel better when they've used more of the credit, and best of all when they've used it all.

In reality, having an unused AMT credit is a good thing. It's an asset that can be used to reduce your income tax in future years. Much of the planning designed to "make full use" of the credit needlessly burns up the credit without producing any compensating advantage. Professional planners sometimes go to great lengths to work out arrangements allowing their clients to avoid having unused AMT credit—by volunteering to pay more tax than necessary.

Calculating the Credit

Working with the AMT credit is a two-step process. First you find out how much credit is *available*, then you find out how much of the available credit you can *use*.

Find the available credit. The first part of your task is to find out how much of the AMT liability from a *prior* year is *eligible* for the credit. This involves recalculating the alternative minimum tax under a special set of rules— sort of an *alternative* AMT. What you're doing here is finding out how much of your alternative minimum tax liability came from *timing* items: items that allow you to *delay* reporting income, as opposed to items that actually *reduce* the amount of income or tax you report. If you're lucky, your entire AMT will be available as a credit in future years. But some people find that only a small portion, or none at all, is available for use as a credit.

For purposes of this book, the most important timing item is the adjustment for exercise of an incentive stock option. This is considered a timing item because the income you report upon exercise of the option for AMT purposes is income you would otherwise report later, when you sell the stock. The fact that this adjustment is a timing item helps you to qualify for the AMT credit.

Most other items you'll get hit with under the AMT don't qualify as timing items, and therefore don't give rise to AMT credit you can claim in future years. In particular, if you encounter AMT liability solely because you had a large long-term capital gain or a large deduction for state income tax, chances are you won't qualify for the AMT credit.

> ▪ Part I of Form 8801 is designed to determine how much AMT credit you have available.

Determine how much AMT credit you can use. If you have some AMT credit available from a prior year, you have to determine how much of the credit you can use in the current year. You can only use the AMT credit in a year when you're *not* paying alternative minimum tax.

The amount of AMT credit you can use is based on the difference between your regular tax and the tax calculated under the AMT rules.

Example: Suppose you have $8,000 of AMT credit available from 2003. In 2004 your regular tax is $37,000. Your tax calculated under the AMT rules is $32,000. You don't have to pay AMT because your regular tax is higher than the tax calculated under the AMT rules. Better still, you're allowed to claim $5,000 of AMT credit reducing your regular tax to $32,000. You can't use the credit to reduce your regular tax below the AMT for the year, though.

In this example, you would still have $3,000 of AMT credit you haven't used. That amount will be available in 2003. In tax lingo, it's *carried forward*.

Of course, you can't claim more than the amount of the available credit. In the example, if the AMT credit available from 2003 was $2,700, then you would use the full amount of the credit in 2004. You would reduce your regular tax to $34,300—*not* all the way to $32,000.

> ▪ Part II of Form 8801 is designed to determine how much of your available AMT credit you can use.

How the AMT Credit Plays Out

How will the AMT credit play out on your tax return? The answer depends on your individual circumstances. The following observations that may help you know what to expect.

To begin with, in normal years most people have at least a little cushion between the tax calculated under the regular income tax rules and the tax calculated under the AMT rules. The size of that cushion depends on many factors, including the number of exemptions on your tax return and the amount of state and local tax you claim as an itemized deduction. For the sake of argument, let's say your *AMT cushion* is $2,000 in a typical year.

The existence of that cushion means you can have at least a small amount of AMT adjustments without incurring any AMT at all. For example, if you exercised an incentive stock option and the adjustment was $5,000, that wouldn't be enough of an adjustment to throw you into the alternative minimum tax, because the amount of AMT on $5,000 is less than $2,000, the amount of your cushion. A $10,000 adjustment would throw you into the

AMT, because this would increase the tax calculated under the AMT by more than $2,000.

It's possible to use some or all of the AMT credit from exercising ISOs without selling the ISO stock.

> **Example:** Suppose you normally have an AMT cushion of about $2,000. In the first year you exercise enough ISOs to incur $3,000 of alternative minimum tax, and this entire amount is eligible for the AMT credit. In the following year you don't have any AMT adjustments: you didn't sell your ISO stock, and you didn't exercise any more ISOs either. In other words, this is a "normal" year for you. In that case, you should be able to claim about $2,000 of your AMT credit, because of your AMT cushion. You would have another $1,000 of AMT credit you didn't use, and that would carry forward to the next year.

Selling some or all of the ISO stock will usually produce a *favorable* AMT adjustment, as explained in Chapter 29, and increase the size of your AMT cushion. If we change the example above so that you sell enough ISO stock in the second year to create a favorable adjustment of $4,000, the AMT cushion would grow to more than $3,000 and you would be able to use the entire credit that year.

Unused credit. You can end up with unused AMT credit even after selling all your ISO stock. This can happen because your favorable adjustment upon sale of the stock is smaller than the adjustment that caused you to pay AMT in the year you exercised the option. As explained in Chapter 29, you can end up with a smaller adjustment because of the AMT capital loss limitation.

> **Example:** You use an incentive stock option to buy stock worth $100,000 for $18,000. You pay $20,000 of AMT, creating an available credit in that amount for future years. The following year you sell the stock for $30,000, and have no other capital gains or losses. Because of the AMT capital loss limitation, your favorable adjustment is only

$15,000 (the difference between the $12,000 gain under the regular income tax and the $3,000 loss allowed under the AMT). As a result you recover only a fraction of the $20,000 available AMT credit.

You can also have unused AMT credit because of a mismatch in tax rates: you pay AMT at 26% or 28% (or up to 35% when the AMT exemption amount is being phased out), but claim the credit against income that's taxed as long-term capital gain at 15%. This is usually a significant issue only for people with very valuable incentive stock options.

> **Example:** You exercise ISOs when the spread is $1,000,000. Your AMT liability from this transaction is about $280,000. The next year, after you satisfied the special holding period for ISO stock, you sell the stock for a price equal to the value of the stock when you exercised the option. For regular tax purposes you report a long-term capital gain of $1,000,000 and pay $150,000 on that gain. The favorable AMT adjustment you receive in the year you sell the stock may allow you to claim only about $150,000 of the credit, leaving $130,000 unused.

The remaining credit will carry forward to future years. Perhaps you'll be able to use it in dribs and drabs over a number of years. When the dollar amounts are large enough, though, it's possible that you'll never recover the full value of the credit.

> • Having unused AMT credit means the tax you paid on sale of the ISO stock was less than the AMT you paid in the year you exercised the option. The remaining credit can produce tax savings in subsequent years.

Part VIII
Vesting

When you receive stock in connection with services you perform, as a stock grant or as a purchase under an option or otherwise, the tax consequences depend on whether the stock was *vested* when you received it. As a general rule, if the stock is subject to a *substantial risk of forfeiture* when you receive it, you won't report income until the risk of forfeiture no longer exists. Your Tax treatment is different—sometimes better, but possibly worse—if you make the section 83b election. This part of the book provides details on the rules that apply when the stock you receive isn't vested.

Part VIII
Vesting

Chapter 31
General Rules for Vesting

It's unfortunate, but one of the most important issues relating to equity compensation is a somewhat technical one that uses arcane terminology. The basic idea here is fairly simple, though. If the company puts certain kinds of restrictions on your right to keep the stock, you don't have full ownership of it yet. That means you don't report income from receiving the stock until the restrictions go away.

Terminology

Here are some words you need to know in working with the vesting rules:

Substantial risk of forfeiture. Only certain types of restrictions will delay the reporting of income. In tax lingo, these are restrictions that create a *substantial risk of forfeiture*.

Vested. If your stock is subject to a substantial risk of forfeiture *and* is not transferable, we say it isn't *vested*. So these are two ways of saying the same thing: if it isn't vested, you have a substantial risk of forfeiture. If you don't have a substantial risk of forfeiture (or the stock is transferable), your stock is vested.

Lapse and nonlapse restrictions. The regulations distinguish between two kinds of restrictions, and give them different tax treatment. Your stock is subject to a *nonlapse restriction* if three things are true:

- The restriction requires you to sell (or offer to sell) your property under a formula price. For example, it may require you to sell for book value, or a multiple of sales or profits.

- The restriction will never go away.

- If you sell or otherwise transfer the stock to someone else, the restriction will apply to that person as well.

Any restriction that doesn't meet the requirements described above is a *lapse restriction*. Notice that a restriction can be permanent and still be a lapse restriction under this definition. Permanency is only one of the requirements for a nonlapse restriction.

Substantial Risk of Forfeiture

There's much confusion about what constitutes a *substantial risk of forfeiture*. Only certain types of risks count here. You may receive stock under circumstances where there's a very real risk that you won't ever get to sell the stock at its current value. Nevertheless, if the risk isn't a substantial risk of forfeiture, you still have to report compensation income *now*. You can't wait until the risk goes away.

Generally, you have a risk of forfeiture under these rules when your right to continue owning the stock depends on whether you continue to work for the company. The most common situation by far is where the company says you'll forfeit the stock (or have to sell it back for less than full value) if your employment terminates before a specified amount of time has elapsed.

A risk of forfeiture doesn't have to relate to a specific time period. For example, it might say you'll have permanent ownership of the stock when sales for your division reach a certain level. You can also have a risk of forfeiture based on an agreement not to compete. Perhaps you received stock in connection with termination of your employment, subject to forfeiture if you work for a competitor of the company within the next two years.

Bear in mind that the risk of forfeiture has to be *substantial*. If it's obvious that the condition for permanent ownership of the stock will be satisfied, the condition doesn't create a substantial risk of forfeiture. Same thing if there's good reason to believe the company won't enforce the forfeiture provision (for example, you control the company). An agreement not to compete may not create a substantial risk of forfeiture if you've reached retirement age or for some other reason have no real ability to compete.

Risk of Decline in Value

A risk that the stock will decline in value is *not* a substantial risk of forfeiture. This is a hard fact for many people to accept, especially if they're unable to sell the stock. You may have a situation where you can't sell the stock for a period of time, and you believe there's a risk the value of the company will decline before you can make a sale. With limited exceptions described in Chapter 32 on restrictions under the securities laws, you don't have a substantial risk of forfeiture in these circumstances. You have to report the current value of the stock as compensation income.

Rules For Vesting

The rules for vesting depend on whether you make the section 83b election. The material in this chapter assumes you did *not* make this election. Chapter 33 provides details concerning the section 83b election.

General. The tax law treats you as if you don't really own stock that isn't vested. You don't report income when you receive the stock. The time before the stock vested doesn't count for purposes of determining whether you have long-term capital gain or loss when you sell the stock. In other words, your holding period begins when the stock vests, not when you received the stock. What's more, if the stock pays dividends, you report compensation income, not dividend income, for any dividends you receive before the stock vests.

Forfeitures. If you fail to satisfy the conditions that create the risk of forfeiture, you forfeit the stock. No doubt you will consider that an economic loss. The stock was yours, and had value, and now it isn't yours any more. As a general rule, though, you can't claim a loss on your tax return. The tax law treats you as if you don't own the stock, and you can't claim a loss for something you don't own.

There's an exception to this rule. If you paid something for the stock, and didn't get that amount back at the time of the forfeiture (or got only part of it back) you can report a loss. This would be an unusual situation, because most companies won't ask you to forfeit the money you came up with to acquire the stock.

Vesting. If things go well, you'll satisfy the conditions to have unrestricted ownership of the stock. At that point the stock is *vested*. You report compensation income at that time, regardless of whether you sell the stock. The amount of income is the value of the stock at the time it vested, reduced by the amount (if any) you paid for the stock.

From that point on, you're treated as if you bought the stock on the date it vested. Even though you may have held the stock for years, you'll have short term gain or loss if you sell the stock a year or less after the vesting date. You have to hold the stock *more than a year after the vesting date* to be able to report long-term capital gain when you sell it.

The *amount* of gain or loss when you sell the stock depends on your *basis* for the stock. Your basis includes the amount of income you report when the stock vests. If you paid anything for the stock, that's included in your basis, too. So your basis is the amount (if any) paid for the stock, increased by the amount of income you report when the stock vests.

Chapter 32
Vesting and Securities Rules

It's possible you'll find yourself holding shares of stock you can't sell, at least for the time being, because of restrictions imposed by the securities laws. That's an awkward position to be in if you have to report income, and pay tax, when you receive your shares. You're likely to wonder if you can postpone reporting the income until the restriction lapses and you're able to sell the stock. With very limited exceptions, the answer is no.

Section 16b

One type of restriction is the *short swing profits rule* imposed by Section 16b of the Securities Exchange Act of 1934. Under this rule you may be required to give up any profits realized from a sale of stock that occurs within six months of a purchase. This rule *does* delay vesting for tax purposes, when it applies. But it doesn't apply very often.

For one thing, Section 16b applies only to certain officers, directors and major shareholders of companies required to file reports to the SEC. That's a small fraction of the people who receive equity compensation. If you're one of those people, you'll know it because the company's legal counsel will have informed you of things you must do—and things you must not.

Even if you find yourself on this short list, you may never have to deal with Section 16b in connection with your equity compensation. One reason is that under Section 16b—unlike the tax law—your holding period begins when you *receive* an option, not when you *exercise* it. If you hold an option for at least six months before you exercise it, you've already satisfied the Section 16b holding period when you receive the stock. What's more, the regulations under Section 16b were revised a few years ago to provide that most grants of equity compensation are exempt.

The bottom line is that Section 16b applies to relatively few people and, when it comes to equity compensation, applies in relatively few situations.

Rule 144

Now we turn to a rule that applies to *many* people who receive equity compensation. If you receive unregistered stock in a public corporation, you're likely to be required to sign an *investment letter* saying you're acquiring the stock for investment and not for resale. The stock certificate will be stamped with a legend indicating it can be sold only in accordance with certain requirements. This stock may be called *lettered stock*, or *Rule 144 stock*.

What's going on here? Companies have to comply with an elaborate (and expensive) registration requirement to bring stock to the market. This assures that investors have access to information that will enable them to make an informed decision on whether to buy the stock. The SEC doesn't want companies to sidestep this process by issuing shares to persons affiliated with the company when those people are going to turn around and sell the shares on the market. Rule 144 establishes rules under which affiliated individuals can receive, and eventually (but not immediately) sell, unregistered shares.

The problem here is that Rule 144 does *not* prevent your stock from being vested under the tax law. Why not? Perhaps because Rule 144 isn't an absolute prohibition on sale. You can't sell your stock on the open market, but you're permitted to arrange a private sale if you can find a buyer who will accept the stock subject to the restrictions of Rule 144.

Then again, a Rule 144 restriction doesn't impose a risk that you'll lose the stock. Your risk is that the stock will decline in value. But the tax regulations specify that a risk of decline in value isn't a substantial risk of forfeiture.

There's one case in which a Rule 144 restriction—coupled with an *additional* restriction imposed by the company—satisfied the court that stock should not be considered vested for tax purposes. I'm not inclined to rely on that case, however. It isn't clear to me that other courts, including the Tax Court, would follow this holding outside the New England states that are included in the First Circuit.

Generally, then, you can't use a Section 144 restriction to delay vesting. You also can't use it to reduce the value of the stock, even though you'll surely have to settle for a discount if you make a private sale before the end of the Rule 144 holding period. About all you can do with Rule 144 is grin and bear it.

Blackout Periods

Many companies impose *blackout periods* in which employees aren't permitted to trade in the company's stock. These periods are timed in relation to the company's quarterly reports. The securities laws don't exactly require blackout periods, but a company that doesn't impose them risks violations. They avoid the implication that employees used inside information to get the better of public investors who don't yet have access to that information. Blackout periods help assure the integrity of the market in the company's stock and can help avoid lawsuits from unhappy investors.

I'm not aware of any ruling that indicates whether such company-imposed restrictions prevent stock from being vested for tax purposes. There can be little doubt of the IRS view, however. The regulations state that property is vested for tax purposes when it is *either* transferable *or* not subject to a substantial risk of forfeiture. It seems reasonably clear that a restriction on transferability, by itself, will not prevent vesting. You need, in addition, a substantial risk of forfeiture. As noted earlier, the regulations plainly state that the risk of property declining in value is *not* a substantial risk of forfeiture. Conclusion: blackout periods don't delay vesting.

Lockup Periods

A similar issue arises as to *lockup periods*. These are periods in which some or all of the existing shareholders are not permitted to sell shares after a company goes public. The securities laws don't impose this requirement; a lockup is imposed by underwriters to make it easier to sell shares that are being offered to the public. As in the case of blackout periods, there is no direct authority on the issue, but the reasoning used above implies that lockups (without some other restriction) don't delay vesting.

Perspective

I hear a lot of frustration from people who feel they shouldn't have to report income from their stock until such time as they're free to sell it on the open market. I sympathize with that feeling. At the same time, there are plenty of people out there who receive stock in companies that aren't publicly traded. Some of these people have no reasonable prospect of selling their stock in the near future, yet they have to report income equal to the value of the stock when they receive it. The point: the tax applies because you received something of value, *not* because you received something you can immediately sell. If you have to pay tax on receiving property you can't sell, you're in an uncomfortable position—but not a unique one.

Chapter 33
Section 83b Election

The tax rules for stock that isn't vested provide both an advantage and a disadvantage when compared to the rules for vested stock. You get the advantage of waiting until the restriction lapses before you report income. If the stock goes up in value while you're waiting, though, you'll report *more* income. A large increase in the value of your stock prior to vesting can have painful tax consequences.

If you don't like the trade-off, you can change the rules. To do this, you file the section 83b election. When you do, you'll be treated (mostly) as if you received vested stock. But you have to act fast: *the election must be made within 30 days after you receive the stock.*

Availability

The election is available when you receive stock with delayed vesting. The point of the election is to treat the stock as if it's already vested, so there's no need to file it if you receive stock that's immediately vested. You might have a situation where it isn't clear whether the stock is vested. In this case you might want to file the election just to eliminate any doubt.

The election is *not* available for *options*. With very limited exceptions, options don't produce current compensation income even if they're vested. Filing a section 83b election when you receive an option doesn't cause you to report current income and, more importantly, doesn't eliminate compensation income when you exercise the option. The election simply doesn't apply to options.

It may apply when you exercise an option, however. Some options impose restrictions so that the stock isn't vested right away when you receive it. In this case it may make sense to file the section 83b election when you exercise the option. See Chapter 34.

Effect of the Election

If you make the section 83b election, you report compensation income when you receive the stock, not when it vests. The value of the stock is determined when you receive it. You have nothing to report at the time the stock vests.

> **Example:** In return for services, you receive 4,000 shares of stock in a startup company. When you receive the stock it isn't vested, and the value is $1.25 per share. Shortly thereafter the company goes public and is hugely successful. When the shares vest two years later they're trading at $50.
>
> Without the section 83b election, you'll report nothing when you receive the shares. When the stock vests, it's worth $200,000 and you'll report that much compensation income. You may pay up to $70,000 in federal income tax as a result.
>
> The result is very different if you file the section 83b election. You would report $5,000 of compensation income when you receive the stock. You have nothing to report when the stock vests. You can continue to hold it without paying another dime of tax. If you sell the stock for $200,000, you'll have a long-term capital gain of $195,000. The tax rate will be 15%, and your total tax may be less than half of the amount you would have paid without the election.

Each Rose Has Its Thorns

The section 83b election doesn't always work out this well. If the stock doesn't rise in value after you make the election, you've *accelerated* tax (paid it sooner) without receiving any benefit. If the stock goes down, you've paid *more* tax than would have been necessary.

Worse, you might forfeit the stock after making the election. In this case you would deduct any amount you actually paid for the stock (subject to capital loss limitation) but you would get no deduction relative to the compensation income you reported when you made the election. That's a miserable result: the election caused you to pay tax on income you didn't get to keep, with no offsetting tax benefit later on.

When the Election Makes Sense

The section 83b election makes sense in the following situations:

- The amount of income you'll report when you make the election is small and the potential growth in value of the stock is great.

- You expect reasonable growth in the value of the stock and the likelihood of a forfeiture is very small.

Conversely, you should avoid the section 83b election where a forfeiture seems likely, or where you'll pay a great deal of tax at the time of the election with only modest prospects for growth in the value of the stock.

Don't miss this chance. You might have to accept a risk of forfeiture on your stock even though you paid full value when you received it. The way this usually works is you agree to sell the stock back for the amount you paid if you quit within a specified period. This is a risk of forfeiture even though you won't lose your original investment. The risk is that you'll lose part of the value of the stock if your employment terminates before the stock vests. *That means that if the stock goes up in value, you'll report compensation income when the stock vests.*

You can avoid this result by making the section 83b election when you buy the stock. In this situation *the election is free.* The election costs nothing because the amount of income you report is the value of the stock minus the amount you paid. You paid full value, so the amount of income is zero. Failure to make this free election can be a costly mistake.

Preparing the Election

There's no special form to use in making the election. You simply put the appropriate information on a piece of paper and send signed copies to the right people. The paper should say "Section 83b Election" at the top and begin with the words, "The taxpayer hereby elects under Section 83b as follows." Then provide the following information:

- Your name, address and social security number.

- A description of the property (for example, "80 shares common stock of XYZ corporation").

- The date you received the property and the taxable year for which you're making the election. (Unless you're one of the lonely few who have a fiscal year, you're making the election for the calendar year in which you received the stock.)

- The nature of the restriction(s) on the stock (for example, "forfeit if employment terminates before July 31, 2006").

- The fair market value at the time you received the stock. Note that for this purpose you can't use the possibility of a forfeiture or any other non-permanent restriction to reduce the value.

- The amount, if any, you paid for the stock.

- A statement as follows: "I have provided copies of this statement as required in the regulation." See below for the copies you have to provide.

Filing the Election

The key point about filing the election has already been mentioned. At risk of repeating myself: *the election has to be filed within 30 days after you receive the property.* If you don't act within that time you're out of luck. You can't wait until you file your return. Here's what you need to do:

- Within 30 days after you receive the stock, send the election to the IRS office where you file your income tax return. (Check the instructions for Form 1040 if you're not sure of the address.) *I highly recommend sending this election by certified mail and getting a stamped receipt with a legible date.*

- Provide a copy of the election to the company that granted the stock.

- In the unusual situation where you had the company transfer the stock to someone other than yourself (such as a trustee), you need to provide a copy to that person as well.

- Attach a copy of the election when you file your income tax return for that year.

> ■ People sometimes forget one or more of these steps and wonder if their election is still valid. It's likely (though not certain) that the IRS will treat an election as valid once you've filed it with the IRS within the 30-day period, even if you failed to follow through with the other requirements.

This is one of those situations where it's very important to keep good records. Make sure you maintain a copy of the election, and evidence that you filed it within the time limit. The value of the stock—and the importance of this election—could grow substantially during the time it takes for the stock to vest.

Chapter 34
"Early Exercise" Stock Option Plans

For many years it has been more or less standard for stock option plans, or the options issued under such plans, to provide for staged exercise of options. In a typical arrangement, you have to wait a year before you can exercise any of your options. At the end of a year, you can exercise 25%, then another year later you qualify to exercise another 25% and so on.

Recently a different approach has gained popularity, especially with startup companies that are planning to go public. These arrangements permit you to exercise all your options immediately. If you do that, however, your stock isn't vested right away. You'll forfeit it (or sell it back to the company at your original purchase price) if your employment terminates within a specified time. Vesting of the stock may be staged in a manner similar to the exercise of options under a more traditional plan—say, 25% per year over four years. Plans with this feature are called *early exercise* stock option plans.

These plans have unique tax consequences. There are no regulations or rulings that spell out the details with certainty. The following description is consistent with positions the IRS has taken in private rulings, proposed regulations and instructions to Form 6251.

Section 83b Election

Early exercise plans are designed to permit you to exercise options at a time when the stock you receive won't be *vested*. Unless you file the section 83b election, you'll report income at the time the stock vests. More importantly, the *amount* of income you report will be based on the value of the stock when it vests. If the value of the stock goes up rapidly between the time you exercise the option and the time the stock vests, you'll report a great deal of compensation income on the vesting date.

These plans are designed with the idea that you may want to exercise the option before the stock has gone up very much—perhaps even immediately after you receive the option. And the expectation is that you'll file the section 83b election. The plan or the option may even *require* you to file the section 83b election when you exercise. That way, you report income at the time you exercise the option—and you won't be hit with a huge tax liability when the stock vests.

> **Example:** You received a nonqualified option to buy 10,000 shares at $0.50 when the company is in its infancy. Now things are looking good. The stock's value is $1, but it will zoom to $5 if the company secures venture capital. In another 18 months the company may go public, and the stock could be at $20 or higher. That would give you a profit of close to $200,000.
>
> If you don't exercise until the stock is at $20, all that profit will be compensation income, taxed at the highest rates. Even if you exercise now, you may have to report most of your profit as compensation income if you don't make the section 83b election. But if you exercise now and make the election, you report only $5,000 of compensation income. Any future growth in the value of the stock will be capital gain. If you hold the stock more than a year, your capital gain will qualify for the favorable long-term rates. Potential tax savings: as much as $40,000 or more.

Special Section 83b Election

There's a little twist on these rules if your option is an incentive stock option, rather than a nonqualified stock option. This type of plan permits you to exercise your option at a time when the stock you receive isn't vested.

The fact that your stock isn't vested has no bearing on your regular income tax. You don't report income when you exercise an ISO, whether the stock is vested or not. Yet it's important that the stock isn't vested—and it may be important for you to do something about it.

Under the alternative minimum tax, exercise of an incentive stock option is treated the same as exercise on a nonqualified option. Under the regular tax, if you exercise a nonqualified option but the stock isn't vested, you don't report income at that time. You report income when the stock vests instead. The same principle applies to AMT treatment of exercise of an ISO.

At first blush that sounds like a good thing. AMT is bad, so why not put it off until another year? The problem here is the same as the problem with nonqualified options under the regular tax. When you postpone the *income* from exercising your option, you also postpone the *measurement* of that income.

> **Example:** Suppose you have an ISO to buy stock at $5 per share. When you exercise the option, the stock is valued at $6 per share. If the stock is vested at that time, you report an AMT adjustment of $1 per share. But let's assume the stock doesn't vest until a year later. During that time the company has gone public and the stock is worth $30 per share when it vests. Now you have to report an AMT adjustment of $25 per share. If you have a large number of shares, that's a big difference!

In dealing with nonqualified options under the regular tax, you can file a *section 83b election* in this situation. You tell the IRS you want to ignore the fact that the stock isn't vested. You'll pay the tax now, and take your chances on possibly forfeiting the stock before it vests. In the example above, if you had a nonqualified option and filed the section 83b election, you would report income of $1 per share when you exercise the option and nothing at all when the stock vests.

As it turns out, you can do the same thing under the AMT if you exercise an incentive stock option when the stock isn't vested. You'll file a *special* section 83b election just for purposes of the AMT. The election will work exactly the same way for the AMT as the regular section 83b election works under the regular tax. You'll report your AMT adjustment in the year you exercise the option, even though the stock won't vest until later. The amount of the adjustment will be determined as of the exercise date. You won't have anything to report at the time the stock vests.

There may be some risk in making this election if you paid substantially less than fair market value when you used the ISO to buy the stock. You could end up paying tax sooner than necessary, and even paying *more* tax than necessary.

The election can produce huge benefits in some cases, however. The earlier example illustrates such a situation. The AMT adjustment at the time of exercise is very small, so there's very little cost in making the election. Meanwhile, the company is planning to go public, with the possibility of a big increase in the value of the stock— and a big increase in the adjustment you report when the stock vests if you don't make the election.

Exercise Immediately?

Early exercise stock option plans invite you to consider the possibility of exercising your option immediately after you receive it. If you do this, your compensation income (or AMT adjustment) should be close to zero, because the exercise price is equal to fair market value at the time the option was granted. You can file the section 83b election (or special section 83b election) described above to avoid having to report any compensation income or AMT adjustment at the time the stock vests. If everything works right, you'll receive the full value of your option while reporting nothing but long-term capital gain. This is why early exercise plans are attractive to some companies, especially ones that are planning to go public.

Sound too good to be true? It isn't, really. To see why, think about what would have happened if your company offered you a different deal. Instead of an option, the company simply said you're allowed to buy some stock right now, paying fair market value, with the stock subject to restrictions so that it isn't vested. This is the type of deal that's described in Chapter 8. You would make the (regular) section 83b election to avoid having to report income when the stock vests. The election doesn't cost you anything because you paid full fair market value for the stock. Guess what? You would be in exactly the same situation as if you exercised an option under an early exercise stock option plan.

There really isn't any magic with this type of plan. In effect, if you exercise immediately you're giving up the benefit of holding an option: the ability to wait and see how the stock performs before exercising. For a mature company with stock price established on the market, you wouldn't be interested in such an arrangement. You'd be better off buying the stock on the open market without any restriction.

The payoff comes with a company that isn't publicly traded. You don't have any way to buy the stock on the market because it isn't available. The only way you can get it is if the company offers you a deal. Getting the kind of a deal described here shortly before the company goes public can be a major bonanza. That's how Margaret Whitman of eBay, Inc. reportedly put herself in a position to save over $100 million in taxes during the Internet boom of the late 1990's

Of course you don't *have* to exercise your options immediately. Particularly if there's some doubt as to whether the company can pull off an IPO (or anything else that will make its value go up), you may want to wait and see. That's the benefit of an option: the ability to get a free look. There's a tax cost if you wait until after the value has gone up a great deal, though, so the "look" isn't completely free.

Part IX
Employee Stock Purchase Plans

Employee stock purchase plans provide a tax-favored way for employees to build an investment stake in their company. These plans are *broad-based*, covering most categories of employees. They often offer a discount of up to 15% of the value of the stock, with the tax consequences of the discount deferred until you sell the stock.

Part IX
Employee Stock Purchase Plans

Chapter 35
Overview of Employee Stock Purchase Plans

Let's make sure we're on the same page. An employee stock purchase plan ("ESPP") is *not* the same as an employee stock ownership plan ("ESOP"). An ESOP is a retirement plan that invests in stock of the employer. This book doesn't cover retirement plans, so we won't be discussing ESOPs.

An employee stock purchase plan is also not an incentive stock option plan. An ISO plan issues incentive stock options. Part V of this book describes the treatment of ISOs. An employee stock purchase plan may issue options, although more often the plan works as a way for you to sign up to buy stock through payroll deduction. There are some similarities between ISO plans and employee stock purchase plans, but the tax treatment isn't the same and it's important to be clear on which is which.

> ▪ Employee stock purchase plans are sometimes called *Section 423 plans.*

Which is which? You should be able to tell which you have by looking at the materials the company provided for the plan. If you don't have those materials, request them from the appropriate office of your company. These materials are important to have in any event.

There are also a couple of tip-offs that you're looking at an ESPP. One is a discount on your purchase. An employee stock purchase plan isn't required to provide a discount, but it *may* provide a discount, and many of them do. An incentive stock option may give you a bargain price if the stock goes up while you hold the option, but you can't get an up-front discount with an ISO. The other tip-off is that the company doesn't have to make ISOs available to all employees. It can give them just to top executives, or to a select group of key people. An employee stock purchase plan can exclude certain people, such as employees who have been with the company less than two years or who generally work fewer than 20 hours per week—but otherwise has to be available to everyone.

A Good Deal

Employee stock purchase plans are a good deal for those who participate. Like incentive stock options, they make it possible for you to buy stock at a bargain price without reporting income until you sell the stock. Yet in some ways employee stock purchase plans are even better than ISOs.

One advantage is that your employee stock purchase plan can provide you with a discount. The purchase price can be as much as 15% below the value of the stock at the time the price is established. Incentive stock options have to be issued with an exercise price at or above the current value of the stock.

The other advantage—and this is a big one—is that you don't have to deal with alternative minimum tax when you buy shares under an employee stock purchase plan. AMT is a major headache in dealing with ISOs. When you buy stock under an ESPP, the AMT doesn't apply.

There's one way an ISO is better, though. Incentive stock options give you the possibility of converting *all* of your profit to long-term capital gain if you hold the stock long enough. By contrast, if you receive a discount on your purchase under an ESPP, you'll have to report some of your profit as compensation when you sell the stock, no matter how long you hold it.

Typical Terms

Employee stock purchase plans are peculiar in that the way they are described in the tax law doesn't match the way most of these plans work. The tax law describes them as plans under which employees receive options. With a few tweaks here and there, an incentive stock option plan could be turned into an employee stock purchase plan.

One of those tweaks is a pretty major one, though. An ESPP has to be made available to all full-time employees on the same basis. Most companies that adopt these plans are so large that it would be difficult to administer a plan where everyone in the company receives ISO-style options. So companies have developed a different way of implementing these plans. Instead of receiving an option, you're offered an opportunity to buy stock at a favorable price through payroll deduction. You can choose to participate or not, and the IRS treats this as an option that meets the requirements for an employee stock purchase plan.

The specifics of these plans vary from one company to the next. The following is an outline of terms that might be considered typical. It's important to check the terms of your own company's plan because those terms may differ in important ways from those described below.

- If you want to participate, you have to sign up by a particular date to have from 1% to 10% of your pay withheld to purchase company stock over a particular *offering period.*

- The money will accumulate for that period of time, and then be used to buy stock at a price equal to 85% of the *lower* of the stock value at the beginning of that period or the stock value at the end of that period. That means your worst case scenario is that the stock price stays the same or goes down, and you buy for 15% below the price at the end of the period. If you're lucky, the stock price goes up, and your bargain will be bigger. For example, if the stock price is $10 at the beginning of the offering period and $15 at the end, the purchase price will be $8.50, which is less than 60% of the $15 price at the time of the purchase. At some companies the purchase price is simply 85% of the stock value at the end of the offering period, regardless of whether the stock went up or down.

- You can back out of the purchase at any time until close to the end of the offering period. (The deadline might be ten days before the end of the offering period, for example, to give the company time to process the paperwork.) If you withdraw from the purchase, the company will refund to you the money that was withheld from your paychecks.

The company doesn't *have* to offer a 15% discount. It can offer a smaller discount or none at all. Notice that you can still come out way ahead without a discount. In the example above, you would be purchasing $15 stock at $10 because the stock price went up during the offering period. If the stock doesn't go up during the offering period and you want to back out of the purchase, you can do so. Be sure to check the plan for the withdrawal deadline. Your only downside if you participate and then withdraw is that you don't get interest on the money that was held in the plan. That's usually a small price to pay for the possibility of buying stock at a bargain price.

■ How valuable is that 15% discount? It turns $85 into $100, and that's a return of over 17.5%. In a typical plan you get that return in six months, so that's an *annual* return of over 35%. But you pay in gradually over the six months rather than having the full amount tied up for that period of time, so it actually works out to an investment return of more than 70%. Of course you can still get burned if you hold onto the stock while it declines in value. See the following chapter for tax strategies.

Chapter 36
ESPP Taxes and Strategies

The beauty of an employee stock purchase plan is that you have nothing at all to report when you acquire the stock. No income on your tax return, and no alternative minimum tax either. When it comes to tax treatment of a valuable benefit from your employer, that's about as good as it gets.

> ▪ I suppose it could be even better. You might want to claim a deduction for the amount of your paycheck that's used to buy the stock. Sorry, but that's not possible. You have to pay tax on that amount, just as if you received it in your paycheck and then used it to buy stock.

When it comes to selling the stock, the tax rules get a little trickier. You're still nowhere near the complexity you have to deal with under the incentive stock option rules, with dual basis and the AMT credit to worry about. But you have to work through some quirky little rules to find out how much of your profit will be treated as compensation income.

Special Holding Period

Just like ISOs, employee stock purchase plans have a special holding period. The tax treatment of your sale will depend on whether you satisfied this test. You meet the holding period requirement on the *later* of the following two dates:

- The date two years after the company granted the option.

- The date one year after you received the stock.

Now we're back to talking about *options*. Under these plans you don't receive an option in the traditional sense, so when does the two-year period start to run? The law doesn't provide a clear answer, but the IRS has taken the position in its private rulings that the two-year period begins on the same date the offering period begins. (Remember that the *offering period* is the time during which the company is taking deductions from your pay, and also the time during which the purchase price of the stock is determined.)

The offering period is often six months, but it can be shorter or longer. If it's less than a year, you'll satisfy the special holding period if you hold the stock until the second anniversary of the start of the offering period. If you receive your stock at least a year after the start of the offering period, the special holding period would be satisfied when you held the stock for a year after receiving it.

> • Any compensation income you have under the rules described below should be reported as wages on your tax return. If the company didn't include this income on your W-2, simply add it to your W-2 income when you fill out your return.

Early Disposition

If you sell the stock, or otherwise dispose of it, before satisfying the special holding period, you have an early disposition (or *disqualifying* disposition). See Chapter 19 for details on what events count as a disposition. The same rules that apply to stock from incentive stock options apply to stock from employee stock purchase plans.

When you make an early disposition you have to report compensation income equal to the bargain element when you bought the stock—that is, at the end of the offering period. The *bargain element* is the difference between the value of the stock on that date and the amount you paid for it.

Example: The stock traded at $10 per share at the beginning of a six-month offering period and $11 at the end of that period, when the purchase occurred. The employee stock purchase plan offers a 15% discount from the lower of those values, so you buy the stock at $8.50 per share. If you sell the stock—or give it away—before satisfying the special holding period, you'll report $2.50 per share of compensation income. That's the difference between the $11 value and the $8.50 purchase price.

You have to report this amount of compensation income even if you don't have a profit on the sale of the stock. (That's a difference from incentive stock options, by the way.) The compensation income increases your basis in the stock, and reduces your capital gain (or increases your capital loss).

Example: In the example above you had to report $2.50 of compensation income. You paid $8.50 for the stock, and this $2.50 would increase your basis to $11 per share. If you sold the stock for $7, you would report a capital loss of $4 per share (in addition to reporting $2.50 of compensation income). If you used the stock to make a gift, you would still report $2.50 of income and the basis of the stock at the time of the gift would be $11 per share.

It's possible, of course, that you'll have a profit on your sale that's larger than the amount of compensation income you reported. In that situation you'll report capital gain in addition to compensation income. The capital gain will be long-term if you held the stock more than a year before the sale.

> - You can hold the stock more than a year but still have an early disposition because the special holding period runs until two years have elapsed from the beginning of the offering period. In that case you still report compensation income as described above but any capital gain or loss you have in addition is long-term.

Example: Same as the previous example, except you sold for $15 per share. Your basis, after adjusting for the $2.50 of compensation income, is $11 per share, so you report $4 per share of capital gain.

Holding Period Satisfied

Now things get interesting. You may still have to report compensation income if you sell *after* satisfying the special holding period. The rule for determining *how much* compensation income to report is a little peculiar.

First, the good news. If you don't have any profit, you don't report any compensation income. That's a much better deal than when you make an early sale. As explained above, you have to report compensation income on an early sale, even if you sell at a loss.

If you sell at a profit, you have to report compensation income. The amount you report is the *lesser* of the amount of your profit or . . . or what? You're probably thinking it's the bargain element again—but it's not. Instead, it's the difference between the stock value *when the option was granted* (which means at the *beginning* of the offering period, not the *end*, when you bought the stock) and the *option price*, which for this purpose is *also* determined as of the beginning of the offering period.

Example: Let's stick with the example we've been using. The value of the stock at the beginning of the offering period is $10 per share, and you buy the stock for $8.50 per share at the end of that period when it's trading at $11. If you sell the stock at $14 after the end of the special holding period, you have to report compensation income equal to the difference between $10 and $8.50, or $1.50 per share. That's less than the $2.50 per share bargain element you would report if you sold before the end of the special holding period. You also report $4 per share of capital gain.

Another: Change the facts. At the end of the offering period the stock is down to $8 per share. The plan says you pay 85% of the *lower* of the price at the beginning of the offering period or the price at the end. That means you pay 85% of $8, or 6.80 per share. The stock's price recovers and you end up selling at $14. You still report compensation income of $1.50 per share, because the bargain element at the time of exercise doesn't matter. You would add $1.50 to your purchase price of $6.80 to come up with a basis of $8.30. Your capital gain on the sale would be $5.70.

If that gives you a headache, you're not alone. Many people get this rule wrong, including the plan administrators at some large companies. There's a worksheet at the end of this chapter that lays out the calculation in simplified form.

Pop Quiz

Feeling smart? Try this one. In the last example above, other things being equal, should you sell before or after satisfying the special holding period? Did you come up with the surprising answer? You do better if you sell early. The amount of ordinary income on an early sale is $1.20, the amount of the bargain element at the end of the offering period. Once you satisfy the special holding period, you have to measure your compensation income as of the *beginning* of the offering period, when the spread was $1.50 per share. The total amount of income is the same in both cases, but an early sale lets you report more of your income as capital gain.

ESPP Strategies

As we saw in the previous chapter, ESPPs are an excellent deal, but there's still the possibility you'll get burned. If the stock goes down while you're holding it, you can lose some of the money you paid to buy the stock. You can also end up with a bad tax result from a disqualifying disposition.

> **Example:** Your company's stock skyrockets during the offering period and you end up buying $50,000 worth of stock for $10,000. Then the value falls to $15,000 and you sell at that price in a disqualifying disposition. You're required to report $40,000 of income. You also have a $35,000 capital loss, but unless you have capital gains from another source you'll deduct only $3,000 of your capital loss, and carry the rest to the following year. You end up paying tax on $37,000 of income even though your profit was only $5,000.

You would avoid this result if you held the stock long enough to avoid a disqualifying disposition. In that case your compensation income would be limited to your actual profit—$5,000 if you sold the stock for $15,000. Continuing to hold the stock exposes you to the possibility of further loss—it can continue dropping below $15,000, and even below the $10,000 you paid to buy the stock. Yet in some circumstances it may be more important to protect yourself from negative tax consequences than to protect yourself from investment loss.

One strategy you can use to avoid this issue is to sell the stock immediately after purchasing it. This isn't what your company had in mind when it offered the plan, so you'll have to check the plan's rules. "Flipping" the stock immediately to secure your 15% profit makes good economic sense if it's permitted but may make the company grumpy. Another plan would be to sell enough of the stock to protect you against economic or tax losses and let the rest ride. That way you're "gambling with house money" and don't risk an actual loss.

If you decide to hold stock from an ESPP, beware of making a disqualifying disposition in a situation like the one in the example above. You may find yourself in a dilemma where the only way to avoid further economic loss is to take the tax hit from a disqualifying disposition, but there are situations where the tax cost of selling now is greater than the amount you're likely to lose by continuing to hold the stock.

Bear in mind that you can have risk of loss even if you plan to sell the stock immediately after buying it. At some companies you won't receive the stock until weeks after the end of the offering period, and the stock can decline by more than 15% while you wait to get your hands on shares you can sell.

Finally, it can be useful to keep in mind the little quirk that sometimes gives you a *better* result from a disqualifying disposition. This happens when the stock went *down* in value during the offering period but then went *up* in value before you sold it (see the "pop quiz" earlier). Even when this happens an early sale may not save you any money because your capital gain may be taxed the same as ordinary income. If your gain is long-term, or if you have capital losses that can absorb the gain, you may benefit from selling before the stock matures.

Tax Calculation Worksheet

You can use the tax calculation worksheet on the following page to determine how much compensation income you have to report when you dispose of your ESPP stock. For an early (disqualifying) disposition, your compensation income is simply the spread on the date you bought the stock, and it doesn't matter how much you received when you sold the stock.

For a qualifying disposition, your compensation income is the lesser of two amounts. One is the spread as of the *beginning* of the offering period. So line 4 is the value on that date and line 5 is the hypothetical amount you would have paid for the stock if you bought it on that date (even though it was impossible to buy it under the ESPP on that date). For most plans, line 5 is 85% of line 4.

The other amount needed for this calculation is determined in lines 7 through 9. According to the tax law, line 7 is the *value* of the stock on the date of disposition. Value can be different from sale proceeds, but IRS Publication 525 refers to the amount of "gain," so it appears you should enter sale proceeds on this line (so that line 9 equals your gain) if your disposition is a sale. Use *value* if you disposed of the stock some other way (for example, by gift).

In all cases, your *basis* for the stock (used to determine how much capital gain or loss you have on selling it) is equal to the amount you paid for the stock increased by the amount of compensation income, if any, reported on the disposition.

ESPP Early (Disqualifying) Disposition

1   Stock value on purchase date (end of offering period)   _____
2   Amount paid for stock   _____
3   Compensation (line 1 minus line 2)   _____

ESPP Holding Period Satisfied (Qualifying Disposition)

4   Stock value at beginning of offering period   _____
5   "As if" stock price (see explanation above)   _____
6   Line 4 minus line 5   _____

7   Sale proceeds or value on date of disposition   _____
8   Amount paid for stock   _____
9   Line 7 minus line 8 but not less than zero   _____

10 Compensation (lesser of line 6 or line 9)   _____

Part X
Option Planning Principles

This part of the book provides background you need for the following section on option planning. Some of the material is fairly basic—Chapter 38 is for people who come to this subject with little knowledge of investing— but there is some fairly advanced material, including details of how to determine the value of stock options.

Part X Option Planning Principles

Chapter 37
General Planning Principles

In planning for how to handle your stock options you may be dealing with large dollar amounts and considerable complexity. To get your planning off on the right foot, follow these guidelines:

Know What You Have

Be sure you have in your possession, and understand the contents of, the documents relating to your stock options. Before you start making decisions about your options you should be able to answer the questions at the end of Chapter 11. Here they are again:

- What is the earliest date you can exercise the option? Does it become exercisable in stages?

- What do you need to do when you exercise the option? Can you borrow to exercise the option? Can you pay the exercise price using stock you already own?

- What restrictions will be imposed on the stock you receive when you exercise the option? Can you sell it right away if you want to? Transfer it to a trust or family partnership? Does the company have the right to get the stock back under any circumstances?

- When will the option terminate? Can you exercise after your employment terminates? What if you die while holding the option?

Without a clear picture of your rights and obligations you may overlook valuable opportunities or make other costly mistakes.

> ■ Every year, many option holders permit perfectly good options to expire even though they are "in the money." An option is a terrible thing to waste!

Give Thought to Your Goals

Financial planning in general should be goal-oriented. Many of your decisions involve a trade-off between risk and possible payoffs. That's especially true when it comes to decisions involving stock options.

Keep in mind that there is no perfect answer to questions about handling stock options. A risk that makes sense for one person may not make sense for another. The context of the risk matters. If a big payoff on your options will change your life for the better, you may be willing to follow a strategy that can lead to that kind of payoff, even if it involves a high risk of loss. The same strategy may not make sense if the benefit of a big payoff is less than the pain that would result from a loss.

Understand the Tax Consequences

Never take a move with your stock options without understanding the tax consequences. Whether you're thinking about exercising the option, making the section 83b election, or selling the stock, you need to have a complete picture of how this will affect your tax return. Often this means looking not just at the year you exercise your option, but also at the following year or years. Tax consequences in the second or third year can change your view of the wisdom of a strategy that looks good based on the first year.

Playing Dice with Tax Money

You may find yourself in a position where you know you will owe a significant tax payment next April, but you have no need to make the payment now. You have a duty, not just to the IRS but also to yourself and your family, to make sure the funds will be available when the tax is due. Too often I've seen people try to gain some fast ground by taking risk with the money they'll need to pay their taxes. That's fine if the risk pays off, but the nature of risk is that it sometimes doesn't.

You can meet with disaster if you exercise an option and hold all the stock. Usually you owe tax when you exercise an option, and even if you've made a tax payment at that time, the payment may not be large enough to cover the tax you owe April 15. It's hard to imagine the stock falling so far that it won't cover your tax liability, but it's happened to plenty of people.

You can get in just as much trouble selling stock at the time you exercise the option if you don't put the tax money in a safe place. It's fun to imagine that money growing dramatically before the tax bill comes due, but any investment that can pay off big in a short period of time—short-term trading, speculative stocks, margined investing—can also lose money rapidly.

From the perspective of the IRS, it's your bad luck, not theirs, if you lose the money you should have set aside to pay your taxes. If you take an action that's going to produce a big tax bill next April, be sure you'll have the money when the time comes. Consider all the risks. Will you be able to pay the tax if your company's stock declines by 80%? If not, you need some money set aside in a safer investment.

Chapter 38
Investing 101

Surveys consistently show a very low level of financial literacy in the public at large. Here are some beliefs held by large segments of the population:

- An investment in stocks is likely to grow over the years at a rate close to 20%.

- My own company's stock is a safe investment because I work there and know what's going on.

- Bonds are likely to produce returns of 10% or more.

- High quality or government bonds are insulated from loss.

- A federal agency protects my investment account against losses.

It isn't surprising that so many people share these and other misconceptions. Few high schools provide training in financial literacy. Colleges may provide this information, but usually only to students taking a business curriculum.

We can't teach you all you need to know to manage your investments in the space available here. For many people the best choice is to consult a qualified financial planner. Our modest goal here is to bring you up to speed on the most important types of investments, and some of the biggest mistakes amateur investors make.

The Big Three

The three main types of financial assets are money market funds, bonds and stocks. You can hold them directly or through mutual funds. These are the core holdings for most investors.

Money market funds. Money market funds or accounts make up one major category of investment. The managers of these accounts invest them in very short-term, low-risk loans to businesses and governments. Investment professionals sometimes refer to these investments as "cash"—they aren't literally cash, but effectively equivalent because you have immediate access and little risk of investment loss.

The problem with these investments is that they produce such low returns that they may not even keep pace with inflation, much less provide genuine growth. Historically, average returns have been less than 4%—and current returns are *much* lower. Think of money markets as a good place to park money you may need on short notice, such as an emergency fund. Better to get low earnings on your money than none at all.

You can open a money market account with many brokers, mutual fund companies and banks. The federal government guarantees certain bank money market accounts against loss, but you're likely to pay for that guarantee in the form of a lower rate of return. Money market mutual funds from reputable mutual fund companies and brokers involve so little risk that the guarantee isn't really important.

If you're setting money aside for a future need, such as taxes you know you'll owe next April, a certificate of deposit can be a good alternative to a money market fund. When you buy a "CD," you're lending money to a bank at a stated rate of interest for a specific period of time.

Bonds. When you purchase a bond, you're buying the right to receive payments on a loan. Many investors have the mistaken belief that bond investments present no risk of loss. Bonds can lose value if it becomes doubtful that the borrower will make the required payments, for example when a company appears to be failing. Even when there appears to be little risk of default (or none at all, in the case of bonds issued by the U.S. Treasury), a bond will lose value if interest rates rise. No one is going to pay $1,000 for your 6% bond if they can invest $1,000 in another bond and get 8% interest. You may find that you can only get $900 for your bond, even though you bought it for $1,000 and it's virtually certain the borrower will make the required payments. That's why you can lose money even on bonds issued by (or guaranteed by) the United States government.

A bond investment gives you more risk of loss than a money market fund. *On average*, bonds provide better returns than money markets (close to 6% historically). That means bonds are likely to be a better choice than money markets for long-term investments. Even if your bonds go through a rough patch, they're likely to do better than money markets over the long haul. When dealing with money you may need in the near future, though, the higher return may not make up for the risk of loss that comes with bond investments. For this part of your wealth it's wise to stick with money market funds or CDs.

You can invest in bonds through bond mutual funds, or you can buy bonds directly. United States savings bonds are available through your local bank, and you can buy Treasury bonds directly from the Treasury. Other bonds, such as corporate bonds and municipal bonds, are available through brokers.

Stocks. Stock ownership gives you a real piece of the action: you become a part owner of the company when you buy stock. For the stocks most people buy (called *common stocks*), stock value grows as the value of the company itself grows. Unlike money market funds and bonds, stocks provide unlimited potential. Historically, investment returns from stocks, including both dividends and capital appreciation, average out to roughly 11%

(before taxes and inflation). That's much better than the 6% produced by bonds, but a lot lower than the guesstimate offered by many amateur investors.

The higher returns of stocks come with higher risk of loss. In the short run, the stock market as a whole can lose 20% or more of its value, and individual stocks can do much worse. In recent years we've seen many companies become spectacularly worthless, and even terrific companies like Intel and Cisco Systems have lost 80% of their value. Despite these risks, the superior returns you can get from a diversified portfolio of stocks make it a great choice for long-term investments, such as retirement savings.

A huge variety of mutual funds provide stock investments of almost any imaginable variety. They may specialize in companies of a particular *capitalization* (a measure of size based on the total value of all outstanding shares), companies in particular segments of the economy such as energy or technology, companies that seem to be growing rapidly (growth stocks) or seem to be selling at a bargain price (value stocks). You can also invest in individual stocks through a broker, making your own choices about what stocks to buy or sell.

Beginning investors are usually better off with mutual funds. They aren't as much fun as picking individual stocks, but mutual funds provide something you simply can't achieve in a regular brokerage account: broad diversification at low cost. We'll have more to say about diversification later.

- Money market funds offer a way to earn modest returns with little risk of loss.

- Bonds offer higher returns, but even "safe" bonds like Treasury obligations can lose value.

- Stocks expose you to still more risk, but over the long run are likely to produce the highest returns.

Asset Allocation

As an investor you have to decide how much of your money to invest in stocks, bonds and money market funds. Financial advisors call this process *asset allocation*. The traditional advice goes something like this:

- Use money markets mainly for emergency funds and short-term investments where avoiding risk of loss is more important than getting the highest return.

- For long-term investments, think first about stocks because they provide the best long-term returns.

- Invest part of your portfolio in bonds to moderate the risks from stock market swings, especially as your investment horizon shortens, but bear in mind that the price of greater safety is smaller expected returns.

Exactly how you divide your investments among stocks, bonds and money markets depends on many factors, including your age, financial goals, and ability to tolerate risk. Some writers suggest formulas for asset allocation, but in the end this is largely a matter of personal choice.

> - Having too much of your money in conservative investments can leave you with dismal long-term performance, while an emphasis on stocks exposes you to short-term swings.

How to Lose Money in Stocks

There are plenty of ways to lose money in the stock market. Many involve dishonesty of some sort. If you're gullible enough to act on chat room comments about a hot penny stock you have only yourself to blame. You can also lose money—*lots* of money—in perfectly legitimate investments. I've seen plenty of people get clobbered, and by far the biggest reasons are:

- Day trading (or other rapid turnover), and

- Failure to diversify

Day trading. If you want to lose money as rapidly as possible, try day trading or some other short-term approach to stocks. Buying and selling stocks rapidly looks like an easy way to pick up extra cash. It's a much easier way to flush money down the drain. Even during the amazing bull market of the late 1990's, more than 90% of people who tried day trading went broke, often within a few weeks of starting. You don't have to be a day trader to lose spectacularly, though. I know a "position trader" (someone who bets on stock moves that are expected within a few days to a few weeks) who went from a multimillionaire to a pauper in just three months. Stocks are great for long-term investing, but short-term trading is a sucker bet.

Diversification. Failure to diversify is an even more common mistake, and one that can be nearly as deadly as day trading. Investors who concentrated their stock holdings in a single stock or sector have been learning painful lessons ever since the market top in early 2000. Diversified investors have seen much smaller declines in the value of their portfolios.

Diversification is a way of reducing risk in your stock investments without moving money to investments like bonds or money market funds that tend to grow at a slower rate. That means a diversified portfolio provides a measure of safety while you continue to enjoy the higher long-term returns provided by stocks. *Diversification reduces risk without reducing the returns you can expect over the long term.*

In a diversified portfolio, the portion devoted to stocks is invested in a wide variety of companies. It isn't enough to invest in a large number of companies. You have to invest in different *kinds* of companies. You can suffer grievous losses if your money is concentrated in a single sector of the economy even though you buy many different stocks in that sector. For example, in a one-year period beginning in March 2000 you could have lost about 65% on an investment in the Nasdaq 100, which is dominated by technology stocks. Over the same period an investment in the S&P 500, a much broader index, declined about 30%. No one feels good about a 30% decline, but it leaves you with twice as much money ($70 out of every $100) as a 65% decline.

We'll have more to say about diversification in the next chapter. The message here is simply to spread your stock investments widely. You can lose money on a diversified portfolio, but the loss is likely to be much smaller than when you concentrate on one stock or sector. Don't risk your financial future on the stock of a single company, including your own company. If you're in love with technology stocks, get over it. Smart investors keep their stock investments broadly diversified.

You can accomplish this in various ways. For many investors the easiest and most efficient way is to invest in stock mutual funds. Bear in mind that many mutual funds concentrate their holdings in particular sectors or types of stocks (such as growth stocks or value stocks) that can go out of favor, leaving you with poor performance. You can avoid this problem by spreading your money among different mutual funds that have different approaches, or by investing in a fund that is designed to mimic a broad stock market index.

■ The most grievous stock market losses are often attributable to rapid trading or failure to diversify.

Chapter 39
A Closer Look at Risk and Return

Investing involves taking risk to obtain returns. Stock options represent extremes: higher than normal risks and, if all goes well, higher than normal returns. In planning for stock options it helps to have a deeper understanding of investment risk and reward.

Stock Prices in a Competitive Market

Everywhere you look, people are trying to tell you which stocks are the best ones to buy. Newspapers, magazines, television, and of course the Internet are loaded with tips about specific stocks or sectors. Books offer to explain how you can pick your own winning stocks. Most of these resources overlook or downplay the way a competitive market adjusts stock prices.

When you think about it, though, it's common sense. If a particular company appears to be a particularly good buy, investors will flock to that stock. Buying pressure will cause the stock price to rise. People will keep on buying as long as the stock is an especially good buy. The buying pressure subsides, and the price stabilizes, only when the price reaches a level where investors believe the stock is no longer a great bargain.

The reverse occurs when a company's fortunes fall. The stock appears to be priced too high, so investors rush to sell it. Selling continues until the price falls to a level where this stock appears to be just as good an investment as any other.

Both of these effects occur very quickly when new information becomes available about a company. Finance professionals managing huge sums keep their fingers on the trigger. News affecting a company can be reflected in its stock price within seconds.

The stock market isn't always right about which companies are going to prosper, of course. Yet at any given time the price represents a collective judgment of the market's participants that at this level the stock is a reasonably good buy: good enough so it makes sense to hold the stock at this price, but not good enough to make it a great bargain, because then buying pressure would drive the price higher. The good and bad news about the company is built into the price.

These price adjustments produce what is known as *market efficiency*. Experts take different views as to how thoroughly efficient the stock market is. Some believe the stock market is efficient enough to make it utterly impossible to pick winning stocks. Others believe skilled analysts can detect and exploit incorrect pricings. Most would agree, though, that markets are efficient enough to make it difficult, even for experts, to predict the near-term performance of particular stocks with significantly greater success than random selection.

For our purposes, the most important implication of market efficiency is this: *there is no way to know whether your company's stock will do well or poorly in the near future.* Perhaps everything is going great at your company. Sales are expanding and profits are rising with no end in sight. That doesn't mean the stock will do well in the future. Investors are aware of how great things are going at your company and took that into account in deciding how much to bid for the shares. The stock's price is at a level where the best minds on Wall Street think it's an okay investment. Not bad, not great. If there were some reason to think the stock offered great returns at minimal risk, buying pressure would cause the price to rise until that was no longer true.

> ▪ A competitive stock market automatically adjusts prices to a level where it's difficult, even for professionals, to tell which stocks are likely to do well.

Return on Investment

Investments can increase your wealth in different ways. Savings accounts and bonds can pay interest. Stocks can pay dividends, and they can also change in value. When we talk about the *return* on an investment, we're referring to the overall change in wealth that results from making the investment, taking into account all these possibilities. For example, if a particular stock pays a 3% dividend and also rises in value by 5%, the return on this stock for the period is 8%.

> ■ Return on an investment is normally expressed in terms of growth per year, taking into account annual compounding. For example, an investment that takes two years to grow 20% has produced a return of about 9.54%—not 10%. If you earn "interest on interest," an investment that grows 9.54% per year will grow 20% in a two-year period.

After-Tax Return

Here's a cliché from the world of investing: *It's not what you make that matters, it's what you keep.* Unless you enjoy paying taxes, your investment strategy should be based on *after-tax* return. That's especially true when dealing with stock options. The tax consequences of strategic alternatives may be vastly different.

> ■ In stock option planning, it's important to focus on the *after-tax return* for your investment strategy.

Expected Return

Determining your return for past periods is merely a matter of crunching numbers. Investment risk means your return for future periods is unknown. For planning purposes it's useful to have in mind the idea of *expected return*. This is the average return we would expect if we made the same investment a large number of times.

If you roll a "fair" pair of dice (where results are random without any bias), the laws of probability tell you the likelihood of each possible outcome. On average, a total of five will occur four times out of thirty-six, while a total of two will occur only once in thirty-six rolls. The "expected return" (average result) for a roll of two dice is seven.

Investments don't work according to the laws of probability. Past performance may give some indication of what we can expect in the future, at least on average.* Yet there are those who will argue that conditions at a particular point in time for a stock, an industry, or the stock market as a whole suggest that future results are likely to differ from past performance. When it comes to stocks and options, we're doubly ignorant: we don't know the exact return we'll receive, and we're not even certain what the probabilities are.

Despite these difficulties, expected return remains a useful concept. We may be able to make comparative judgments about two investment strategies, even without knowing exactly what return to expect from either of them. We may conclude, for example, that the after-tax expected return for one strategy is higher than for another, and we may even be able to estimate *how much* higher. That information will help us decide how far to tilt in favor of a particular strategy.

> • Expected return is an estimate of the average return we would get if we made the same investment a large number of times.

Risk

What is investment risk? For most people the first thing that comes to mind is the possibility of losing money.

---

* For a fascinating look at how stocks have performed in the long run—and fluctuated in the short run—I highly recommend *Stocks for the Long Run* by Jeremy J. Siegel.

That's certainly an important risk to consider, but investment professionals take into account other types of risks. Investors sometimes think an investment is "safe" even though it has *liquidity risk* (the risk you can't convert it to cash when the need arises) or *inflation risk* (the risk that the investment return won't keep pace with inflation). Depending on your circumstances, these can be as important as the risk you'll lose money on an investment.

Our main focus here will be on the kind of risk investment professionals call *volatility*. That's a fancy word for the up and down movements of stocks. A downward fluctuation may result in a loss, and that's probably the main reason for thinking volatility is undesirable. Yet there's more to the concept of volatility.

> ▪ While there are various kinds of investment risk, the kind we will focus on is *volatility*, the tendency of an investment's value to fluctuate.

Volatility

Although most would agree that risk is bad, many investors seek out volatility, often without realizing that is what they're doing. Test yourself with this question:

> If two investments have the same expected return, but one has a greater chance of providing a *superior* return, which one is better?

Many people will choose the investment that gives greater chance of a superior return, without stopping to think that this choice also, *by definition*, has the greater likelihood of doing poorly. Remember that expected return is the *average* of all results. If two investments have the same expected return, then the only way one can provide a better shot at superior results is to also have the greater risk of producing losses.

So let's ask the same question a different way. Suppose two investments have the same expected return, so that *on average* they'll produce the same results. One has higher volatility than the other: a greater chance of very good or very bad results. Which is the better investment?

It turns out there isn't an answer to this question that fits all situations. For one thing, risk itself has some psychic value for many people. People who gamble in casinos or play the lottery usually do so because they find risk is fun, not because these activities are a good way to make a profit. Some people (though certainly not all) get a similar kind of enjoyment from holding risky investments. Even if you don't think of yourself as a gambler, you might prefer "interesting" investments to "boring" ones, at least for some of your money.

The answer to the question also depends on context. Various factors—wealth, youth, personal disposition—may make it easy for you to shrug off a loss, leaving you inclined to accept more risk as the price for a chance at bigger gains. If your circumstances or personality make losses seem especially painful, you'll want to choose safer investments.

Generally, risk is bad for your financial health. Because of the mathematics of compound interest, a volatile investment may not produce as much wealth even if the average annual return is the same.* What's more, many investors find it difficult to handle the stress that can result from holding volatile investments. They may abandon a sound investment plan at precisely the wrong moment (after a nosedive and before an upturn). Even if they can hang tough, all that stomach churning may make them wonder if it was worth it.

When we're talking about large dollar amounts, as is often the case in dealing with stock options, the main reason to focus on volatility is that it can lead to massive losses. I have seen option holders lose millions because they didn't fully appreciate how much volatility risk they were taking. If you're comfortable with the risk of having

---

* Simple example: after two years, an investment that produces a steady 10% return would grow by 21%, which is better than one year of zero return followed by a year of 20% return (or vice versa).

nearly all your net worth tied up in stock options, or in your company's stock, that may be indication you don't fully appreciate the extent of that risk.

That doesn't mean you should always choose the strategy that involves the least risk. Often that's also the strategy that provides the smallest rewards. If your choices involve strategies with different levels of risk, consider what you have to gain from making the riskier choice. It could make sense to accept a moderate increase in risk for a strategy that involves a much higher expected return. Taking higher risk without a greater expected return—what investment professionals call *uncompensated risk*—doesn't make sense.

Even when risk appears to be compensated by the promise of higher returns, you should avoid strategies that include the risk of life-altering losses. A strategy that makes sense for 20% of your assets may not make sense for 90% of your assets. Too many option holders act as if they have to figure out which strategy is best and follow that strategy for all their options. In many cases the wise choice is a split decision, so you can benefit from the riskier strategy if it pays off but avoid financial disaster if it goes down in flames.

- Some degree of risk is necessary to achieve investment rewards.

- Avoid *uncompensated risk*—risk that doesn't come with a probability of higher rewards.

- Also avoid risks that leave you exposed to the possibility of major financial disaster.

- The best choice between two strategies is often a split decision.

How Risk Relates to Return

This view of risk plays out in the way the markets price financial assets. For example, when a company seeks to raise money by issuing bonds, investors buying those bonds will consider the financial soundness of the company. If the borrower looks shaky, investors will demand a higher rate of interest. Generally speaking, investors won't accept the greater risk of buying bonds from a financially weak company unless they receive compensation in the form of higher expected return.

Historically, stocks have been riskier investments than bonds, at least when held for short periods of time. Stocks have also provided higher long-term returns than bonds. That result is consistent with the notion that risk is undesirable. When it appears that stock prices have reached levels where the expected returns don't justify the risk, investors move their money to safer investments. Stock prices fall to a level where investors believe the returns that can be expected in the future justify the risks of holding stocks.

As a general rule of investing you have to take higher risk to have a chance at higher returns. If an investment appears to offer a high rate of return with very little risk, investors will be attracted to that investment. They will continue buying until the price rises to a level where the expected return is in line with the apparent risk. That's the main reason you should be skeptical whenever someone suggests that a particular investment offers an exceptional return at little or no risk. If the risk were really that small, investors would have bid up the price until the return was no longer exceptional.

> ▪ As a general rule, investments that produce higher returns involve greater risk. Safer investments generally provide smaller returns.

Risk Is Relative

Suppose you're evaluating a particular investment and find it has unusually high volatility: the price moves up and down more than most other investments. If this were the only investment you planned to own, that might be a good reason to consider buying something else. You own other investments, however, and on taking a closer look you discover a curious fact: the price of this investment doesn't tend to move in the same direction as your other investments. It often goes up when the others go down, and vice versa. Considered by itself, this is a risky investment, but adding it to your holdings may actually *reduce* the overall risk of your portfolio because of the way the ups and downs often cancel out.

You aren't likely to know the precise level of risk for a particular investment or the way that risk correlates with your other investments. Yet it's important to have this concept in mind when mapping out an investment strategy. It isn't just the amount of risk that matters. What's important is how an investment affects the overall risk of your portfolio.

For example, suppose you're following a strategy that involves holding a big chunk of your company's stock. That means you're exposed to risk specific to that company and also risk relating to that industry and sector of the economy. One way to moderate that risk is to make sure your other investments are heavily weighted *away from* that industry and sector. For example, if you work for a high tech company, your other investments would emphasize companies *other than* high tech. That approach increases your chances of having gains that offset your losses if the company's stock goes sour.

> ▪ Evaluate the risk of an investment or a strategy in relation to your overall portfolio, not in isolation.

Diversification

This brings us back to the subject of diversification. We stated in the previous chapter that this is a way to reduce risk without reducing expected return. It's helpful to understand why that is.

Suppose your stock portfolio consists of a single stock. That stock may lose value if any of the following occur: the company falls on hard times, the industry in which the company operates suffers, or the stock market as a whole declines. Now suppose you divide your portfolio among various companies in that industry. If the original company falls on hard times your portfolio won't take such a big hit; in fact, it may not take any at all because the company's problems may result from successful competition from others in the industry. You're still exposed to an industry downturn and to anything that affects the stock market as a whole.

If you take things a step further, dividing your portfolio among stocks in different industries, you manage the risk that's specific to any one industry. You still bear the risks of the overall stock market—you're stuck with those risks if you want to participate in the superior long-term returns you can get from stocks—but overall your risk is far smaller than if you didn't diversify.

The year 2000 provides a perfect example. Stocks as a whole were off that year, but investors who diversified broadly throughout the stock market suffered less pain than others. Those who restricted their investments to particular industries, like telecom or the Internet, saw their portfolios decimated. Many who held only a single stock were wiped out entirely.

What's amazing about diversification is that it doesn't have to reduce your expected return. You can have less risk of loss without diminishing the overall long-term performance of your portfolio. The risks of individual stocks partially cancel each other out, but the expected return for the portfolio will be a weighted average of the expected returns of the stocks that make up the portfolio. If you diversify from a single stock into a group of stocks that all have about the same expected return, you end up with a portfolio that has less risk without any loss of performance.

If you fail to take advantage of this opportunity, you're taking *uncompensated risk*. Remember, our general rule is to take added risk only if we get something for it other than the excitement of seeing our investments go up and down. Investors who fail to diversify are taking more risk than necessary for the returns they receive.

There are various ways to diversify. You can select individual stocks to add to your portfolio, or obtain the services of an investment advisor to do so. You can invest in a mutual fund where the fund manager selects the stocks. Another choice is an index fund: a mutual fund that seeks to mimic a stock index such as the S&P 500. No single approach is best for everyone, so you can choose based on your investment philosophy.

Whatever approach you use, be sure to have a wide variety of stocks from different industries. If you rely on mutual funds, beware concentration in particular industries or sectors. A mutual fund that invests only (or primarily) in technology stocks, for example, may seem sexier than a broader fund, but it won't provide the full benefit of diversification.

> ▪ Whenever possible, use diversification to reduce risk without reducing expected return.

Your Company's Stock

The stock of the company where you work is a special case. Most people recognize this, but for the wrong reason. According to surveys, many people believe their own company's stock represents a smaller risk than other stocks, or even a diversified portfolio. The truth is exactly the opposite. Your own company's stock is the riskiest investment you can make.

Concentrating your holdings in *any* single stock is a bad idea. As explained earlier, diversification allows you to reduce your risk without reducing your expected return. When you invest in the stock of a single company you take uncompensated risk.

If the stock happens to be the company where you work, the risk is even greater. What happens if the company does poorly? Your stock loses value, the same as if you invested in some other company. At the same time you may face other financial problems. Companies that are doing poorly often have to reduce their workforce.

Your job could be in jeopardy just at the time your investment is tanking. Even if you hold onto your job, the company may not be in a position to hand out bonuses and raises. By investing in your own company you increase your economic exposure to problems the company may suffer.

It's natural to want to invest in your own company. You gain some comfort from knowing what's going on there. You may feel you should own some of the stock out of loyalty. That's fine, but don't gamble your entire financial future on your company's stock. Even excellent companies sometimes see their stock decline by 80% or more. Workers at those companies don't predict those collapses any better than ordinary investors. If anything, faith in their own company seems to make it harder for them to recognize a bad situation that's obvious to outsiders. Use this simple rule when dealing with any single stock, including the stock of your own company: invest as much as you can afford to lose.

Stock Option Planning in Context

Your stock options are, of course, indirectly an investment in your own company's stock. As we'll see, they involve even greater risk than stock because of built-in leverage. I'm not suggesting you abandon them for this reason. The greater risk comes with a potential for higher return—in some cases, spectacularly higher return. Up to a point, it makes sense to bear the added risk for the possibility of greater performance.

At the same time you should do what you can to moderate that risk. If your options give you huge exposure to your company's stock, you should minimize any other exposure you have in your 401k account or other investments. As you consider strategies for your stock options, think in terms of risk and reward, and be prepared to accept somewhat smaller rewards in situations where that choice will produce significantly lower risk.

Chapter 40
Option Economics and Valuation

At first glance, options seem pretty simple. It's easy enough to understand the basic deal: they give you the right to buy stock at a specified price. There's a lot more to the story, though. In fact, the 1997 Nobel Prize in economics went to two people who worked out methods to determine the value of stock options.* You don't need to know all the math behind option valuation, but you'll be in a better position to handle your options correctly if you gain a better understanding of option economics. In this chapter we'll start with the basics and then wade just far enough into the theory to let you make informed judgments about your options.

The Profit Profile

The profit profile of an option shows how your profit relates to the price of the company's stock. For an option you receive from your employer, the profit profile is simple and intuitive. It's built on two facts:

1. You don't have to exercise the option if the stock value is lower than the strike price.

2. You didn't pay anything for the option, so there's no loss if you simply allow the option to lapse.

It's easy to see that you have no profit or loss from the option at a time when the value of the stock is less than the strike price specified in the option. Likewise, you can

---

* The prize went to Robert C. Merton and Myron S. Scholes. The prize announcement also acknowledged the contribution of the late Fischer Black.

see that your profit from the option is $1 per share for every dollar the stock value rises above the strike price.

At the option's expiration date, you'll let it lapse if the stock value is at or below the strike price. That means you don't care *how far* below the strike price the final stock value might be. If the stock value is above the strike price, you will exercise the option, and in that case it certainly does matter *how far* above the strike price the stock value has risen.

> ▪ Options provide profit equal to the difference between the stock value and the exercise price, with no loss on a stock value below that price.

Options Compared to Stock

One way to understand the value of a stock option is to compare the economics of holding the option with the economics of buying the stock right away for the same price. Both situations permit you to benefit from growth in the stock's value. The option provides two additional benefits.

1. As an option holder you're protected against a decline in stock value below the strike price of the option. The option acts like an insurance policy that protects you from losses you might bear if you held the stock.

2. As an option holder you don't pay the purchase price until you exercise the option. In effect, you get an interest-free loan because you pay later, even though you're participating in the growth of the stock right now.

At the same time, some stocks provide a benefit you don't receive as an option holder: dividends. Much of our discussion will proceed with the implicit assumption that your company's stock doesn't pay dividends. In Chapter 42 we'll see that your decision to continue holding an option may be affected if the stock pays dividends.

> • The key point here: options provide the equivalent of an insurance policy and an interest-free loan.

Leverage, Risk and Options

When you borrow to make an investment, you increase your profit potential—and your risk of loss. Suppose you buy real estate worth $100,000 for $10,000 down and a $90,000 loan. If you later sell it for $105,000 (a 5% increase over what you paid) your profit of $5,000 is *50%* of the $10,000 you invested.* By the same token, a 10% decrease in the selling price would leave you with a loss of *100%* of the amount you invested. Because of this multiplier effect, debt incurred to make investments is called *leverage.*

We mentioned above that an interest-free loan is implicit in an option. That means an option is like a leveraged investment. If you have an option to buy $100,000 worth of stock for $90,000, you can cash out for $10,000 by exercising the option and selling the stock. A 5% increase in the value of the stock will increase the amount you can cash out by 50%, while a 10% decline in the stock price eliminates your ability to turn your option into cash.

An option's leverage is highest when the value of the stock is close to the exercise price of the option. In this range, relatively small changes in the value of the stock can produce wide swings in what we call the intrinsic value of the option (see below). As the stock price moves farther above the exercise price of the option, the interest-free loan becomes a smaller percentage of the stock value. Leverage decreases, and changes in the value of the option track more closely changes in the value of the stock.

---

* For the sake of this simple example we're ignoring *many* important factors, including depreciation and interest on the loan.

Intrinsic Value and Time Value

One of the principal questions facing option holders is when to cash out. We'll consider this question in detail in Chapter 42. The answer depends largely on how the value of your option breaks down between *intrinsic value* and *time value*.

Intrinsic value. The "obvious" part of a stock option's value is called *intrinsic value*. This is the difference between the current value of the stock and the exercise price of the option. For example, an option to buy stock at a price of $12 per share has an intrinsic value of $4 per share when the stock is trading at $16. Intrinsic value is never negative because you wouldn't exercise an option when you can buy the stock more cheaply in the stock market. The intrinsic value of "under water" options is $0.

Time value. Intrinsic value doesn't account for the entire value of a stock option. It's easy to see this if you think about an option that is exactly "at the money"—for example, an option to buy at $12 per share when the stock is trading at $12. This option has no intrinsic value, but you know intuitively that its value is more than zero. The option represents a valuable economic right. We don't know if you'll ever realize a profit from the option, but the *possibility* of receiving this profit is worth something.

Even an option that's *out of the money* has value. If you have a $14 option on stock that's currently trading at $12, there's still a possibility you'll profit from the option. This option has less value than a $12 option on the same stock, but it still has some value.

This portion of a stock option's value relates to the amount of time left until the option expires. Other things being equal, an option that has three years left to run is more valuable than an option that will expire next week. We call this portion the *time value* of the option.

Time value can be seen as the value of being able to delay purchasing the stock. As noted earlier, an option provides an implicit insurance policy, freeing you from risk of loss relating to a drop in the stock value below the exercise price. An option also provides you with an interest-free loan, permitting you to delay paying for the stock until you decide to exercise the option. These two built-in elements of an option combine to create its time value.

> ▪ The value of an option consists of two elements: *intrinsic value* (the difference between the current value of the stock and the exercise price) and *time value* (the value of being able to delay purchasing the stock).

The Optionee's Dilemma

In some ways, options you receive from your company are similar to options that trade in the options markets. Both permit the holder to buy shares of stock at a specified price if and when the holder decides to exercise the option.* Both have the kinds of value described above: intrinsic value and time value.

Option traders are aware of time value and for this reason rarely exercise an option until just before expiration. When you exercise an option, you receive only the intrinsic value. The time value disappears because the option no longer exists. An option trader would rather *sell* the option than exercise it. The buyer will pay for the intrinsic value *and* the time value. As long as an option has time left before expiration, it makes more sense to sell the option than to exercise it.†

It's rarely possible for workers to sell the options they receive from their company. Your only choices are to exercise the option—giving up the remaining time value—

---

* In the markets, an option to buy is a *call* option. The markets also trade *put* options that permit the holder to *sell* shares at a specified price.

† There's an exception for options on stocks that pay dividends, where the remaining time value of the option is less than the dividend you can receive by exercising the option.

or continue holding the option and risk losing its intrinsic value.

This is what I call the *optionee's dilemma.* Whatever intrinsic value your option has acquired can disappear faster than you can say "irrational exuberance." It makes sense to think about cashing in so you can diversify your holdings. Yet that means abandoning the remaining time value of your option. To protect the more tangible intrinsic value of your option you have to destroy the more abstract, but potentially lucrative, time value.

You can see now why it's important to get a handle on the two components of option value. If your option has tremendous intrinsic value and very little time value, it may make sense to exercise the option and sell the stock. When the time value of the option predominates, you're likely to be more inclined to postpone exercising, even knowing that the intrinsic value could disappear.

> ▪ Exercising an option gives you the ability to secure the intrinsic value, but at the cost of the time value.

Valuing Your Options

It may not be possible to determine the precise value of your stock options. One problem is the difficulty of determining the stock's volatility, a key factor in option valuation. The term of the option is also likely to be uncertain. The option may have five years to run, but what if your employment terminates? What if your company is acquired? Events like these can cut off the life of your option before the stated expiration date.

Fortunately, for planning purposes you aren't likely to need a precise value. A rough idea will be enough to tell you whether your option is ripe for harvesting (see Chapter 42). The key is to have a realistic estimate of the overall value so you can determine how much time value you abandon when you exercise your option.

The most reliable way to determine the value of an option is to consult with a financial planner who's familiar with these calculations. If you want to try the calculation on your own, various web sites provide online option value calculators. If you prefer to set up your own spreadsheet to make these calculations, instructions telling how to do this appear later in this chapter. Whether you use an online calculator or your own spreadsheet you'll need to understand the factors that go into the calculation.

Current price of the stock. This one is easy enough. You can get the current price from a newspaper or the Internet.

Exercise price. Normally this is easy to find also. It should be in your option agreement. Many companies also provide summaries or online services that let you know the exercise price of your options. Note that the exercise price may be adjusted in the event of a stock split or similar corporate transaction.

Time to expiration. Usually you need to enter this factor as a number of years. For part of a year, you'll have to divide the number of months by 12 or number of days by 365 (for example, you would enter 2.36 for an option that expires two years and 131 days from now). If your option has many years to run and you think it's likely that some event (such as your decision to switch jobs) will prevent the option from running its full course, use a reasonable estimate of how much longer the option will run instead of the official expiration date.

Interest rate. This is supposed to be the "risk-free" interest rate. That's usually assumed to mean the rate on U.S. Treasury obligations for the relevant term. A higher interest rate increases the calculated value, but small changes in this figure won't affect the value of your option enough to have a significant impact on planning. You can choose a reasonable value and you'll be close enough. In this book we use 5% as the risk-free interest rate.

Dividends. As the holder of an option, you miss out on part of the benefit of holding the stock: you don't receive dividends. Larger dividends mean smaller option value.

Some calculators call for you to enter the annual *dividend yield*. That's the value of the stock divided by the annual total for dividends. For example, a $30 stock that pays a quarterly dividend of $0.15 per share has a 2% dividend yield (annual dividend of $0.60 per share divided by $30). Other calculators may ask for the quarterly dividend and the date of the next dividend payment.

Volatility. This factor is sometimes called the *standard deviation* of the stock's price. Higher volatility increases the value of an option. In other words, an option on stock that goes up and down a great deal is more valuable than an option on stock that remains relatively steady. This factor can affect the value of your option quite a bit, yet it's a difficult factor to determine. Volatility isn't "observable" in the sense that you can look it up.*

Experts can calculate the *past* volatility of a stock, but that won't necessarily tell you the precise value to put in the option valuation formula. Different methods can result in different answers. How far back do you look? How do you break down the lookback period (days, weeks, or some other period)? How do you handle extraordinary events? Even if there were general agreement on how to determine past volatility, the calculation wouldn't tell us what we really want to know: how much volatility should we expect in the future? Volatility can change. One study found, for example, that the average volatility for the stocks making up the S&P 500 fell from about 47% as of November 30, 2000 to about 39% a year later—a change that can make a big difference in option values.† This change in volatility is distinct from the drop in prices that occurred over the same period.

An expert may get a better estimate of future volatility by looking at the prices people pay in the options markets for options on the same company's stock. By plugging in the other factors that determine the value of an option it's

---

* Volatility is *not* the same as *beta*, another measure of risk that sometimes appears in stock data tables.
† These figures are from the January 2002 issue of *The Executive Edition*, a publication of HayGroup.

possible to "solve backwards" for the volatility. This *implied volatility* method should be more accurate than relying on past volatility because it tells you in effect what finance professionals are estimating as the future volatility of the stock. Not all stocks have publicly traded options, however. Even when implied volatility is available, it will usually pertain to a period much shorter than the period of your option. Studies have shown that implied volatility can vary depending on the time remaining before expiration of the option.

As a practical matter, for option planning purposes you aren't likely to need a very precise figure for volatility. You may be able to find figure that's good enough for this purpose in your company's annual report. Publicly traded companies generally include information about stock option valuation, including volatility assumptions, in the footnotes of their financial statements. If you can't dig up a volatility number this way you can make a reasonable guess by using the following guidelines:

- The volatility of a large, mature stock is likely to be between .2 and .5.

- If your company is large but attracts the kind of attention that makes for a bumpier ride, or is reasonably stable but smaller, the volatility is likely to be between .4 and .8.

- Companies that attract speculative trading, particularly in the tech sector, can have volatility of 1.0 or higher.

Any calculation using a crude estimate of volatility will provide only a crude estimate of the value of your option. If your situation calls for an accurate estimate, you may need to consult with an expert who can narrow the range for this factor. In many situations you can develop a strategy for handling your options without a precise calculation of value.

A Simple Black-Scholes Spreadsheet

The following instructions can be used to set up a spreadsheet to calculate option values according to a modified version of the Black-Scholes formula.* These instructions assume you have a version of the Excel spreadsheet program that includes the NORMSDIST statistical function. Here's what your spreadsheet will look like:

	A	B
1	Stock price	100
2	Exercise price	90
3	Interest rate	0.05
4	Volatility	0.6
5	Time to expiration	2.5
6	Dividend yield	0.02
7		
8	d1	0.6645
9	Option value	40.212
10		
11	Intrinsic value	10
12	Time value	30.212

Simple Black-Scholes Spreadsheet

Begin by entering labels in column A as indicated. Expand column A so these labels don't run over into column B, where you will type the actual numbers.

The first six numbers in column B are the variables that determine an option's value under this formula. Note that for "Interest rate" you would enter "0.05" for 5% interest. Similarly a 2% dividend yield is entered as "0.02."

---

* The original formula does not take dividends into account. The formula used here makes a rough stab at this problem, treating dividends as if they were paid in a constant stream.

The figure labeled "d1" is an interim calculation used in the option value calculation. The formula for cell B8 is:

`=(LN(B1/B2)+(B3-B6+B4*B4/2)*B5)/(B4*SQRT(B5))`

The formula for "Option value" in cell B9 is:

`=B1*EXP(-B6*B5)*NORMSDIST(B8)`
`-B2*EXP(-B3*B5)*NORMSDIST(B8-B4*SQRT(B5))`

Now cell B9 should provide the value of an option when appropriate figures are entered in cells B1 through B6. As a check, try entering the numbers in the figure above to see if you get the same results.* The formulas for the last two numbers are simple. The formula for intrinsic value in cell B11 is:

`=MAX(0,B1-B2)`

The formula for time value in cell B12 is:

`=B9-B11`

Intrinsic value is the part of the overall value you would be able to cash out if you exercised the stock option now and sold the stock at its current value. The time value of the option is simply the total value (given by the modified Black-Scholes formula) reduced by the intrinsic value.

If you play with different values in this formula you'll see how the different factors affect the value of an option. The formula reveals that an option that's "at the money" (where the stock value is the same as the option price) may have significant value. Even an option that's slightly out of the money can have significant value, but as you would expect the formula assigns little value to an option that's far out of the money unless volatility is high and the option has a long time until expiration. You'll also see that as the stock price rises above the exercise price the time value of the option decreases (although not as rapidly as the intrinsic value increases). Mathematically, the time

---

* If your results don't match, one thing to check is whether you used the NORMDIST function instead of the NORMSDIST function.

value of an option is highest when the stock price is the same as the exercise price.

> ■ Don't rely on values generated by this spreadsheet without confirming them with a financial advisor.

The Formula

Those who have enough math background to work with logarithmic and statistical functions may be interested to see the function calculated by the spreadsheet described above. Here it is:

$$C = S e^{-\delta T} N(d_1) - K e^{-iT} N(d_2)$$

In this equation, the symbol N stands for the probability of a normally distributed variable (with mean of 0 and variance of 1) having a value less than the following expression (d_1 or d_2). The symbols d_1 and d_2 stand for these expressions:

$$d_1 = \frac{\ln(S/K) + (i - \delta + \sigma^2/2)T}{\sigma\sqrt{T}}$$

$$d_2 = d_1 - \sigma\sqrt{T}$$

The variables represent the following values:

S = current stock price

K = exercise price of the option

i = risk-free interest rate

σ = volatility of the stock

T = time to expiration

δ = dividend yield as an annual percentage

Part XI
Planning Your Option Exercise

This part of the book digs into some serious planning issues. Applying the planning principles of the previous part and the tax rules discussed earlier in the book, we'll examine different types of situations to uncover strategies that work—and some that look good but turn out to be unrewarding.

Part XI Planning Your Option Exercise

Chapter 41
Nonqualified Options and Capital Gain

Suppose you have a nonqualified option that still has plenty of time to run. You're confident the stock price is going to rise, and it occurs to you that this increase in value will end up being taxed as compensation when you exercise the option. That means paying the highest income tax rates. Wouldn't it be smarter to exercise the option *now* and hold onto the stock? That way the price increase you're expecting will produce a capital gain. If you hold the stock more than a year, you'll have *long-term* capital gain and pay federal tax of only 15%.

It turns out that if your company's stock is *publicly traded*—meaning you can buy and sell shares in the stock market—this strategy isn't so smart. Even when you have complete confidence the stock price will rise, you're better off continuing to hold the option. That seems like a strange conclusion, but it follows from some fairly simple logic explained below. We'll work from the assumption that you have an option to buy 1,000 shares at $10 per share. You plan to sell the stock when it reaches $110—an increase of $100 per share, or $100,000 overall—and expect that will happen by the time your option expires. To make things simple, we'll also assume any compensation income you receive is taxed at a combined state and federal rate of 40%, and capital gains are taxed at a combined state and federal rate of 20%. That means you end up with $60,000 after tax if you wait until the stock reaches $110 before exercising the option.

Zero Spread Exercise

One possible strategy is to exercise the option when there is no gain at all. You're hoping to capture *all* your profit as long-term capital gain by exercising when the market price of the stock is $10 per share. That's a high-risk choice because you lose money if the stock price drops at all, but we're assuming your confidence in the stock is strong enough to make you comfortable with that risk. If things go as planned the stock will rise to $110 while you hold it more than a year. When you sell it, your $100,000 profit will be long-term capital gain. You end up with $80,000 after paying the 20% state and federal capital gains tax. This strategy appears to be better than holding the option while the stock price climbs to $110: on an after-tax basis you end up with $20,000 more.

Yet there's a fatal flaw in this reasoning. You would be foolish to exercise the option when you can buy the stock in the market for the same price. Using $10,000 to buy stock in the market doesn't expose you to any greater risk than using the same amount to exercise the option. The profit is the same, too, and so is the tax. Buying the stock in the market puts you in the same position in every respect except one: you still have the option. So when the stock reaches $110, you sell the stock for a profit of $100,000 (taxed at 20%) *and* you cash out the option—exercise and sell the stock—for *another* $100,000 of profit. The second $100,000 is taxed as compensation at higher rates, of course, but you are *far* better off than if you exercised the option when the stock price was $10.

> ▪ For publicly traded stock, it doesn't make sense to exercise a nonqualified stock option that isn't in the money.

Midterm Exercise

So far we've learned that it doesn't make sense to exercise the option at the very beginning of its journey from $10 to $110. What about exercising halfway through that journey, when the stock is at $60? That way you capture at least *some* of your profit as long-term capital gain, while avoiding the mistake of exercising the option when you could have bought the stock in the market for the same price.

What's wrong with this plan? When you exercise the option you have to come up with $30,000: $10,000 to pay the exercise price plus another $20,000 to pay the 40% state and federal tax on your $50,000 profit. Remember, with a nonqualified stock option you have to pay this tax even if you don't sell the stock. When you factor in the need for this $30,000, this "midterm exercise strategy" becomes unattractive.

Sell to cover. One way to come up with this money is to "sell to cover." At the time you exercise the option, you give instructions for the immediate sale of enough shares to pay the exercise price and the tax. We're doing all this when the stock is trading at $60, so you need to sell 500 shares—half your holdings—to come up with the $30,000. You hold the other 500 shares until the stock price reaches $110 and then sell. You receive $55,000 in the sale (500 shares times a value of $110) and pay $5,000 capital gains tax,* leaving you with $50,000. Remember, though, you would have had *$60,000* if you simply held the option until the stock price reached $110. Using a "sell to cover" approach to convert future appreciation to long-term capital gain is a losing proposition.

Using other funds. Perhaps you don't have to sell to cover. You're able to come up with $30,000 to exercise the option and pay the tax without selling any of the stock. Using this approach you'll end up selling 1,000 shares for a total of $110,000. You have to pay $10,000 capital gains tax on this sale, and you came up with $30,000 when you exercised the option, so your net with this approach is $70,000. That's $10,000 *more* than if you waited until the stock reached $110 to cash in your option.

---

* You had $25,000 of capital gain as the value of the stock rose from $30,000 to $55,000, so at 20% your tax is $5,000.

The problem here is a variation on the problem with the zero spread exercise discussed earlier. The $30,000 you used to exercise the option would have produced a bigger profit if you used it to buy shares in the market. With that much money you could buy an additional 500 shares. When the stock reaches $110 you sell those shares for $55,000. After paying $5,000 capital gains tax you have a profit of $20,000. We saw earlier that you can gain $10,000 in after-tax profit by using your $30,000 to exercise the option. Using the $30,000 instead to buy stock gives you twice that benefit, a profit of $20,000.

The point here is not to suggest that you should actually buy more shares of stock. Buying additional shares only adds to an already high level of risk you have relating to your company's stock. The analysis is designed to show that exercising an option on publicly traded stock to qualify for capital gains rates on future appreciation is not as desirable as it might appear.

> ▪ The "midterm exercise strategy" does not maximize the after-tax profit from your stock option.

Conclusion

The surprising conclusion of all this analysis is that the best strategy in this situation is the one that ends up making you pay the most tax. The leverage provided by continuing to hold the option is more powerful than the benefit you can achieve by taking advantage of the lower tax rate for long-term capital gains. Here are some important limitations on this conclusion:

Option expiration. The analysis above assumes your option has plenty of time to run at the time you're planning your strategy. The decision process when the option is about to expire is different. In that situation it could make perfectly good sense to exercise an option that's in the money and continue to hold the shares because you believe the stock price is likely to rise.

Normally it makes more sense to sell some or all of the shares to diversify, but for entirely different reasons.*

Incentive stock options. Incentive stock options provide added tax benefits that encourage you to hold the shares after exercising the option. For analysis, see Chapter 43.

Privately held companies. The arguments presented above rely heavily on your ability to buy stock in the market. That opportunity doesn't exist for companies that are not publicly traded. This is why many pre-IPO companies offer early exercise stock option plans, permitting option holders to exercise before the stock is vested. As discussed in Chapter 46, the strategy of exercising to hold pre-IPO stock is risky but potentially rewarding.

When to cash out. Our general conclusion here is that if you have a nonqualified stock option on publicly traded stock and the option still has time to run, you shouldn't exercise the option until you're ready to cash out by selling the shares. But when should you cash out? Should you wait until the option is about to expire, or does it make sense to exercise the option and sell the stock at some earlier time? We address this question next.

---

* See Chapters 38 and 39.

Chapter 42
When to Harvest Your Options

If your options are *in the money*—the stock value is greater than the exercise price—you'll want to exercise them at some point before they expire. But when? Should you hold on until the bitter end, hoping to squeeze every last bit of value from your options? Or should you take some money off the table earlier to reduce your risk?

Harvesting Options

In this chapter we use the word "harvest" with intentional ambiguity. Determining that your options are ripe for harvesting doesn't necessarily mean you'll immediately exercise all of them and sell the stock. When your options are ready for harvesting, you may want to cash them in gradually over a period of time, and in the case of incentive stock options you may want to hold some or all of the stock long enough after exercise to avoid a disqualifying disposition. Our immediate issue is determining when to start that process—in other words, when your options are ripe for harvesting.

The Optionee's Dilemma

Options give you the opportunity to build wealth more rapidly than with more conventional investments. Yet the wealth you've built can slip away with astonishing speed. Even at the best companies a sudden drop in the stock price can occur without warning. The built-in leverage of stock options magnifies that risk.

> **Example:** You have an option at $40 to buy stock valued at $60. If the stock price falls 20% to $48,

the intrinsic value of your option falls 60%, from $20 to $8.

You can protect the profit that's built into your option by exercising it and selling the stock. After subtracting the amount used paid to exercise the option and paying the tax you're left with an amount we can call the *cash-out value*.

> **Example:** You have an option to buy $100,000 worth of stock for $30,000. If you exercise the option and sell the stock you'll have a pre-tax profit of $70,000. After paying tax of $28,000 you're left with $42,000, the cash-out value of the option.

Harvesting your option allows you to protect the cash-out value of your option from SDS: sudden disappearance syndrome. Yet in most cases, cashing in before the end of the option's term means giving something up: the remaining value of your option. To protect part of the value, you have to throw another part of the value away. That's what I call the *optionee's dilemma.*

There are two pieces to the value you discard when you harvest an option that still has time to run. One is the tax advantage from continuing to hold the option. As we'll see below, even a nonqualified stock option provides a tax advantage relative to conventional investments.

The other thing you lose when you exercise an option earlier than necessary is its remaining time value. As explained in Chapter 40, time value is a two-part benefit. It's the value of being able to benefit from any future increase in the stock's price without having paid for the stock (a built-in interest-free loan) and without being exposed to loss attributable to a decline in price below the exercise price of the option (a built-in insurance policy).

When you harvest a stock option that isn't about to expire, you gain relative safety for the cash-out value of your option, and you give up the benefits of continuing to hold the option. The remainder of this chapter will help you identify situations where the value you abandon when you harvest an option is small relative to the benefit of being able to reinvest the cash-out proceeds.

> ▪ Perhaps you're thinking of spending the cash rather than reinvesting. Understanding the value of the benefits you abandon when you harvest your stock option will help you make an informed choice in this situation, too.

Predicting Stock Prices

It's natural to think the decision about when to harvest your options should be based on, or at least affected by, your view (or *someone's* view) of whether the company's stock is likely to rise or fall in the near future. You're thinking you'll feel like an idiot if you cash in your options just before the stock breaks out for a big advance. Likewise you'll kick yourself if you hold on while the stock price plummets. You may be inclined to seek an expert opinion from your financial advisor, or perhaps try to develop your own opinion, reading analysts' reports or gleaning information from the Internet.

The simple fact is that you don't know where the stock price is heading in the near future and neither does anyone else. As explained in Chapter 39, the stock market automatically adjusts the price of each stock to a level where investors judge the stock to be a reasonably good investment—not a great one or a terrible one. If there were good reason to expect the stock price to leap up or down in the near future, the leap would have already occurred as investors bought or sold to take advantage of that information. That makes it impossible to predict short-term price movements with consistent accuracy.

Feel free to read commentary about your company. You're likely to find it interesting and you may learn something useful. One thing you certainly won't learn: where the stock price is headed in the near future. "Target prices" and other predictions by analysts aren't worth the electrons that display them on your computer screen.

Likewise, you can't predict where the stock is going by looking at where it's been in the past. Traders like to say the trend is your friend, but identifying the trend and knowing when it has changed requires the arts of a sorcerer. The best assumption to make about the near-term future of your company's stock is that it may go up or down from its current price, and either possibility is about equally likely. And no matter how good you feel about the company or its stock, be sure to consider the possibility that the stock price could suddenly go down *a lot*. No company is immune to that risk.

Risk and Return

That doesn't mean the decision about when to exercise your options is simply a guessing game. Instead of trying to figure out which way the stock price is going to move, you need to focus on the option itself. Does it provide an enhanced return? If so, *how much* enhanced return? Is it enough to justify the risk of letting the option ride?

> **Example:** Suppose you have an option to buy 10,000 shares of your company's stock at $17.00 per share. The option won't expire for three years, and the stock is currently trading at $17.10.

You can cash in the option and have a pre-tax profit of $1,000. It's possible you'll never see that $1,000 if you don't act now. Yet you probably suspect this isn't a wise move, and in this case your instinct is correct. Without knowing anything about your company we can suppose there's a reasonable chance the stock will rise to $20.00 or more within three years. If that weren't a good possibility, the stock wouldn't be trading now at $17.10. Harvesting the option now lets you move the $1,000 (or what's left after you pay your taxes) to a safer investment, but at the cost of a realistic opportunity for a profit of $30,000 or more.

> - In the end your option may expire worthless with the stock price languishing below $17.00. If that happens you shouldn't feel you made a mistake when you decided to let it ride. You made the best choice with the available information. In the risky world of investing, bad results can come from good choices. The key is to avoid bad choices: strategies that expose you to risk without adequate reward.

Highly Appreciated Options

In the example above, the stock value had grown only a tiny bit above the exercise price of the option. That factor made it easy to see it was unwise to exercise the option years before expiration. Let's turn now to the opposite situation, where the exercise price is such a small fraction of the value of the stock that it might as well be zero. The wisdom of harvesting these options is less obvious.

The discussion below assumes you have an option to buy $100,000 worth of stock for $0. As usual we make the simplifying assumption that your compensation income is taxed at a combined state and federal rate of 40%. For the moment we'll also assume the stock does not pay dividends. Later we'll see how dividends affect the analysis.

Value of the option. When you exercise an option that isn't about to expire, you abandon the remaining time value of the option. That's one possible reason to delay harvesting an option. Strangely, when the exercise price of an option is zero, the time value of the option is also zero. It doesn't matter how much time is left until the option expires.

One way to understand this is to notice that the intrinsic value of the option—the difference between the stock value and the exercise price—is $100,000, the same as the value of the stock. If the option had time value in addition to intrinsic value, the option would be worth *more than* the stock. Yet the option is simply a right to receive those shares, so it can't be worth more than the stock.

Here's another way to look at it. The time value of an option consists of an interest free loan and an insurance policy. If the exercise price is zero, the amount being loaned is also zero, so the loan has no value. Likewise, insurance against seeing the price of the stock dropping below zero has no value.

The value you abandon when you exercise this option is zero. This means you have no reason to delay harvesting the option unless the tax benefits of continuing to hold the option are great enough to justify the risk.

Tax deferral. The most obvious tax benefit of continuing to hold the option is *deferral*. If you harvest the option now, you'll have to report the $100,000 spread as compensation income. At an assumed 40% rate you would pay $40,000 in income tax, leaving you with a cash-out value of $60,000. You might expect to gain a benefit by delaying exercise of the option. It seems the longer you can put off paying this tax, the better.

Surprisingly, there is little or no deferral benefit in this situation. You can see this if you compare two situations: holding this option versus holding $60,000 worth of the stock. Suppose you hold for three years and the stock price doubles during that period. If you held $60,000 worth of stock, it would double to $120,000. With the option instead, you would cash out for $200,000, pay $80,000 in tax and end up with exactly the same amount: $120,000.

Normally you can profit from deferring payment of $40,000 to the IRS. You invest the money during the deferral period and any earnings are yours to keep, subject to regular income tax rules. You don't get that benefit when you delay harvesting a stock option, though. In effect, the entire investment return on the deferred tax goes to the IRS. It's as if they already own 40% of the option, even before you exercise it.

You may eke out a limited deferral benefit by delaying exercise of your option. The value of that benefit depends on whether you're subject to withholding on the compensation income you report when you exercise the option and whether you're required to pay estimated tax to make up the part of the tax that isn't covered by withholding. If you're thinking of exercising an option in December, you may find an advantage in waiting until January. Yet waiting a full year, or several full years, to exercise this option will not provide a deferral benefit.

Capital gains. So far we've come up empty in our search for reasons to delay harvesting a highly appreciated option. You don't give up any time value when you exercise it, and the apparent benefit of tax deferral turns out to be largely a mirage. There remains a tax benefit for continuing to hold the option, however. It relates to capital gains when you sell the stock.

Return to the comparison between holding the option and owning $60,000 worth of the company's stock. We saw that in either case, if the stock doubled during the holding period you end up with $120,000 worth of stock. When you harvest the option, you end up with $120,000 *after tax.* If you sold stock after it doubled to $120,000, you would have to pay tax on a $60,000 capital gain. At a combined state and federal capital gains rate of 20% you would owe $12,000. Holding the $100,000 option is like owning $60,000 worth of a special kind of stock where capital gains are tax-free.

Risk and return. We noted earlier that options can magnify the risk associated with changes in the stock price. That isn't true when the exercise price of the option is zero. The value of this option will change directly with the value of the stock, dollar for dollar. Holding the option provides an enhanced return (because we avoid paying capital gains tax on a future increase in value) without increased risk. That means, for a stock that doesn't pay dividends, you would rather hold the option than hold the stock.

Normally you're more interested in knowing whether holding the option is better than moving to some *other* investment. Holding a concentrated position in the stock of a single company exposes you to uncompensated risk you can avoid by diversifying.* Other things being equal, you're far better off when no single stock represents a large portion of your net worth.

Other things are not quite equal when you hold a highly appreciated option instead of stock. In effect, the option gives you the benefit of tax-free capital gains. In my judgment this is not a great enough advantage to justify the risk of keeping a large portion of your wealth tied up in the company's stock. Here's why.

We can't predict how your company's stock will perform, but we know that over the long haul, stocks appreciate by about 10% per year on average. Assuming state and federal capital gains tax will claim 20% of that return, the annual expected return for a typical stock on an after-tax basis would be about 8%. Holding the option allows you to avoid capital gains tax on growth in the value of the stock, so the after-tax return for the option is the same as the pre-tax return of 10%. The option permits you to boost your expected return from the stock by about two percentage points.

Investment professionals know that a difference of two percentage points compounded over a long period of time can make a huge difference in the wealth you accumulate. In this case, though, we aren't adding two percentage points to your long-term return. Instead, we're adding two percentage points to your short-term expected return. That's not enough to justify the risk you take when you remain undiversified. Two percentage points of increase in expected return is not adequate compensation for the high risk associated with having a large portion of your wealth concentrated in a single company's stock.

> ▪ An option this deep in the money is ripe for harvesting. The benefit you can expect from continuing to hold the option is small in relation to the benefit of diversifying.

---

* See Chapter 39.

A suggested approach. Figure out how much of your wealth you would hold in your company's stock in a neutral situation where you're investing from scratch with cash. Experts recommend a small percentage: some say no more than 10% and others use an even smaller number. Then consider how much (if any) you should increase that number because of the small boost you get from avoiding capital gains tax on appreciation that occurs while you hold the option.

Now look at your overall investments, including 401k and other retirement savings. How much are you already exposed to your company's stock? Is there room for further exposure in the form of a stock option? If the answer is *no*, because a big share of your other wealth is tied up in this stock, you should strongly consider harvesting the entire option to diversify your holdings.

If the answer is yes, come up with a figure for the amount of stock you want to hold through ownership of the option. Divide that number by .6, because you really own only 60% of the stock covered by your option. The IRS effectively owns the other 40%. The resulting number tells how much of your option you should retain. The rest you should harvest to make diversified investments.

> **Example:** Your option is deep in the money and has a bargain element of $100,000. You decide it makes sense to hold $12,000 worth of the company's stock through your option. Divide that number by .6 to find that you need $20,000 worth of option to have the equivalent of $12,000 worth of stock. You harvest $80,000 worth of your option, using the after-tax proceeds to diversify, and continue to hold the remaining $20,000 worth of your option.

Stocks that pay dividends. So far we've assumed your company's stock doesn't pay dividends. That's important because if it *does* pay dividends you have less reason to continue holding the option. In fact, you might be better off holding the stock than holding the option.

Shareholders receive dividends, but option holders don't. As long as you hold your investment in the form of an option, you're missing out on part of the return from a stock that pays dividends. A highly appreciated option on stock that pays dividends can actually have *negative* time value.* There's no economic benefit in continuing to hold such an option.

To evaluate the impact of dividends on your options, you need to know the stock's *dividend yield* (see Chapter 40). Any number much over 1% pretty much wipes out the small capital gains advantage in continuing to hold a highly appreciated option. You should strongly consider harvesting such an option.

Moderately Appreciated Options

We saw earlier that an option isn't ripe for harvesting when it's just barely in the money unless it's about to expire. Then we examined options that are so deep in the money that the exercise price might as well be zero. We found that you give up very little when you exercise these options, so it makes sense to harvest at least a portion of them to diversify your holdings. Now we turn to the middle cases, where the option has built up a spread that's large enough to be worth protecting, but the exercise price remains a significant part of the option value.

Value of the option. The single most important factor here is how the value of your option breaks down between intrinsic value and time value. When the intrinsic value—the part you can convert to cash—is small relative to the time value you should be more inclined to gamble on continued holding of the option. When the reverse is true you should be thinking of harvesting your options.

---

* In theory you should exercise an option when its time value falls to zero, so true negative time value exists only if you're prevented from exercising at that time.

Earlier in this chapter we presented an extreme example of the first situation. The exercise price was $17.00 and at a time when the option had three years to run the stock was trading at $17.10. You could cash in all 10,000 shares for a profit of $1,000, but that approach doesn't seem to make sense because the profit potential of the option is many times that amount.

The option valuation formula confirms our intuition. It tells us the theoretical value of this option is nearly $60,000.* Exercising now to secure the profit of $1,000 means abandoning more than $50,000 of time value. In this extreme case we were able to choose a strategy even before we knew the value of the option. In other situations calculating the value will help make an informed decision.

Theoretical but real. The valuation formula tells us approximately how much you would expect to receive if you sold the option in a market where options of this type were freely traded. No such market exists, so you may be tempted to believe the value is too theoretical to be useful. Yet the value generated by the formula represents an average of the statistically likely outcomes. An option valued at $60,000 may yield profit of $200,000 or no profit at all. We don't know what the actual profit will be, but we know the average payoff on this bet is $60,000. That makes it a pretty good bet if the amount we're gambling is $1,000—and a poor one if we're gambling $59,000.

Discounting the time value. Although there's an economic reality behind the theoretical value of your option, it may be appropriate to act as if the time value is smaller than the amount calculated in the formula. We can justify that approach by considering what someone would pay to be in your situation. Anyone considering a purchase of your option would have to take into account the option's *lack of marketability*. In other words, you won't pay full value for an investment if there's no

---

* We arbitrarily chose a volatility factor of 0.5 for this calculation.

convenient way to get out of it by selling it to someone else. If you were buying such an option, you would also reduce the purchase price based on uncertainty about some of the factors. It's hard to know what volatility factor to use, and in most cases there's a risk the option will expire early for some reason such as termination of employment.

The time value of an option is *real*, but the theoretical value generated by the formula is greater than the amount someone would pay to be in your shoes. When thinking about how much time value you abandon by harvesting your option, it makes sense to discount the value generated by the formula. The size of the discount is somewhat arbitrary. A discount in the range of 30% to 50% seems appropriate, but a number outside that range could make sense if your situation makes the option a particularly suitable investment—or a particularly unsuitable one.

A suggested approach. Deciding when to harvest a moderately appreciated option is inevitably a judgment call. In effect you have to weigh the benefit of the relative safety you can achieve by cashing in your option against the potential profit you leave on the table by abandoning the option's time value. Understanding the time value can help you make an informed decision, but your choice can also be influenced by personal factors such as your other investments and your appetite for risk.

> **Example:** The total exercise price of your option is $200,000 and the current value of the stock is $300,000. The option has three years left to run, and you're considering whether to cash in your $100,000 profit now or continue to hold the option.

The value of this option depends on the volatility of the stock and other factors that go into the valuation formula (see Chapter 40). Plugging in reasonable values might yield an option value of about $160,000. The *intrinsic value*—the part you can cash in—is $100,000, so the *time value*, according to the formula, is $60,000. Applying a reasonable discount to that figure, you decide it's realistic to think of the time value as being something like $40,000.

The question you're faced with is whether to abandon $40,000 worth of time value to gain access to the $100,000 you can obtain by harvesting your option. There's no right or wrong answer to that question. Your choice may depend on whether you already have other wealth in diversified investments, how close you are to retirement, how comfortable you are with risk, and a variety of other factors. Analysis of the option's value doesn't determine your strategy, but it helps you understand the economic consequences of your choices.

The best strategy isn't necessarily all or nothing. Most stock options permit partial exercise. Given the risks involved and the subjective nature of the decision, it can make good sense to take advantage of that opportunity.

Timing Issues

We saw earlier that you can't predict short-term moves in the price of your company's stock. As a consequence you have no way of knowing whether you're harvesting your options at a good time. How will you feel later about the decision you made today? Will a decline in value make you wish you exercised sooner? Or will the stock shoot up, making you wish you waited longer?

There's no way to eliminate the potential for regret. You can moderate that risk somewhat by cashing in your options in stages. Even if you've decided all your options are ripe for harvesting right now, you may want to divide them into three or four batches and exercise each one separately with an appropriate time period in between. Decide in advance that you'll exercise one batch every ten days (or whatever period you choose) to reduce the chance of unlucky timing for the entire option. In a sense, this is a form of diversification: diversifying over time periods instead of different investments.

You may also want to fine-tune your timing to take into account differences in tax years. In some cases it's best to exercise all your options in one year (for example, to avoid phasing out your personal exemptions in multiple years) and in other cases you do better when you spread them over multiple years, to reduce the amount of income that's taxed in the highest bracket. Multiple-year tax projections can be helpful in developing your strategy.

Chapter 43
Exercising ISOs to Hold the Stock

ISOs provide a special benefit if you hold the stock after exercising the option. Under the regular income tax you don't have to report income until you sell or otherwise dispose of the stock, and if you hold the stock long enough your profit on sale of the stock will be long-term capital gain. These benefits are offset by the requirement to pay AMT in the year of exercise and the risk of holding a concentrated stock position for at least a year. In this chapter we look at the economics of holding ISO stock. Is it worth it?

It Depends

You knew I was going to say that, right? The answer depends on where the balance tips between the tax benefit you can expect to obtain if you hold the shares, and the diversification benefit you get from selling the shares right away. There isn't any formula that allows a direct comparison between the two, but we can gain some insight into the tax benefit and then draw some general conclusions.

Three Big Factors

There are three big factors that determine how much tax benefit you get from holding the shares. One is your tax bracket, the second is a number I call the *profit percentage* of your stock option, and the third is the AMT impact.

Tax bracket. The benefit of holding ISO shares comes from converting ordinary income to long-term capital gain. That means your potential benefit is greater when you're in a higher tax bracket. In the 25% tax bracket, you're reducing your tax by 10 percentage points when you qualify for the 15% capital gains tax. In the 35% tax bracket you save twice as much, reducing your tax by 20 percentage points. It can be worthwhile to hold ISO shares when you're in the 25% or 28% brackets, but the benefit is greater when you move up the ladder.

> ▪ Bear in mind that your normal tax bracket won't necessarily apply to all your option income. If you exercise an option with a large bargain element, the income can push you into a higher tax bracket.

Profit percentage. An even more important factor in determining whether to hold shares is something I call the *profit percentage* of your stock option. This is the bargain element of the option divided by the total value of the shares at the time you exercise it. For example, if your option allows you to buy $100,000 worth of stock for $15,000, the profit percentage is 85% (bargain element of $85,000 divided by $100,000 share value). When the profit percentage is high, the benefit of holding the shares is greater because you don't have a lot of money tied up in the stock. When the profit percentage is low, you get less bang for your buck (and have more risk of loss) when you hold the shares because you have more money invested.

AMT impact. The third big factor determining the tax benefit from holding the shares is the AMT impact. This varies depending on which of the following categories apply to you:

- You can exercise the option and hold the shares without paying any AMT at all.

- You'll pay AMT if you hold the shares, but you can expect to recover the full amount of AMT as a credit in the following year.

- You're unlikely to recover the full amount of AMT as a credit.

Exercising Without AMT

Unless you're already paying AMT for some reason, you can probably exercise at least some ISOs without paying AMT. If you're like most people, the amount of bargain element you can harvest this way is probably no more than $5,000 or $10,000. Whatever the number may be, you can reap a better tax benefit from those shares than you'll get if you have to pay AMT.

That doesn't necessarily mean you want to hold all the shares you can without paying AMT. If the profit percentage for your option is on the low side, you might be taking too much risk for the amount of tax benefit you can expect. Yet if your profit percentage is high, these are the shares that give you the greatest tax advantage.

> **Example:** You're in the 28% tax bracket and have an option that allows you to buy $10,000 worth of shares for $2,000. Running a tax projection, you find that you can hold the shares without paying AMT.

Holding the shares ties up the $2,000 you used to exercise the option and exposes you to the risk that some or all of your $8,000 profit will disappear. Yet it also will allow you to reduce your tax rate on the profit from 28% to 15%. Because the profit percentage of the option is so high (80%), the tax benefit translates into a healthy boost in your expected return—an increase of 17 percentage points over a normal investment, by my calculation. That means this could be a risk worth taking, if your overall financial situation is such that you can afford to maintain this much of an investment in your company's stock.

AMT Credit Recovered

Many people find themselves in a situation where they have to pay AMT in the year they exercise an ISO, but can reasonably expect to recover the full amount of the tax as an AMT credit when they sell the shares a year later. When that happens, the total amount of tax you save by holding shares is the same as if you never paid AMT in the first place. Yet you incurred more risk, and also got a somewhat diluted benefit because you had to pay the tax one year and recover the credit the next year. These factors reduce the overall benefit of holding the shares by about one-third. Holding the shares can still make sense when the profit percentage is high, especially if you're in a high tax bracket, but in marginal cases the reduced benefit may lead you to sell immediately after exercising the option.

Unrecovered Credit

You may find that you aren't able to recover all your AMT as a credit, especially if your ISO has a large bargain element. If you don't recall how this can happen, review the example at the end of Chapter 30. In this situation, you may receive some future benefit from the AMT credit, but only up to a point. When the unrecovered AMT credit becomes so large that there is no reasonable prospect of using it all, there is no further tax benefit in holding the shares.

Recent changes in the tax rates have a significant effect on where the benefit of holding ISO shares drops off. If you have an incentive stock option with a very large bargain element—say, more than a few hundred thousand dollars—you're likely to find that there's little or no tax benefit in holding more than half the shares. In fact, when the numbers get large enough so we can disregard details that are normally significant (like your tax bracket), the tax benefit drops away when you hold more than 35% of the shares.

> **Example:** You were in the right place at the right time and now find yourself ready to exercise an ISO that has a bargain element of $4,000,000. You're prepared to hold some of the shares but only up to the number that will provide a tax benefit.

If you hold all the shares, you'll pay about 28% of the total, or $1,120,000, in AMT. Assuming the stock price remains unchanged, you'll have a $4,000,000 capital gain next year. The regular income tax on that amount is $600,000 but you'll recover $600,000 in AMT credit. The bottom line for year 2 is that you used part of the credit to avoid paying $600,000 *more* tax. So you didn't pay more tax that year, but you also didn't really get anything back when you recovered part of the credit. The total amount of tax you paid is still 28% of the total. You're left with a huge unused (and almost surely unusable) AMT credit.

Now suppose you hold just 35% of the shares, and sell the other 65% immediately after exercising the option. Your regular income increased by $2,600,000 (65% of $4,000,000). The regular income tax on that amount is $910,000. Under the AMT your income went up $4,000,000, because your AMT income includes income from the shares you held *and* income from the shares you sold. That means the tax calculated under the AMT rules is still up by $1,120,000. You end up paying $910,000 in regular income tax and $210,000 in AMT in the year of exercise. If we assume you sell the remaining shares a year later with no change in value, you'll have a capital gain of $1,400,000, exactly enough (at the 15% capital gains rate) to soak up $210,000 in AMT credit.

Okay, those numbers are confusing, but here's the main point. The benefit of holding ISO shares comes from converting regular income (taxed at rates up to 35%) to capital gain (taxed at 15%). But when the numbers get big, the AMT steps in and says your total tax is never going to be less than about 28% of the bargain element. The best you can do is shave seven percentage points (from 35% to 28%) off the amount of tax you'll pay on this income. How many shares do you have to hold if you want savings equal to seven percentage points? The answer is 35% of the shares.* You can't get more tax benefit by holding

---

* Mathematically, this is (a) the difference between the regular tax rate of 35% and the AMT rate of 28%, divided by (b) the difference between the regular tax rate of 35% and the AMT rate of 15%. It's pure coincidence that it comes out equal to the top tax rate of 35%.

more shares. All you do is build up an AMT credit you're unlikely to use.

ISO Tax Benefits in Perspective

As always, you have to evaluate these tax benefits in the context of the amount of risk it is appropriate for you to take. Just because you can get a tax benefit from holding shares doesn't mean that's the right choice for you. It might make sense, in light of your financial condition and personal preferences, to hold fewer shares or none at all after exercising an incentive stock option.

On balance, though, it often makes sense to hold at least some of the shares. The tax benefit can boost the return of the shares by 20% or more, so that if the stock goes up 10% you get an after-tax return equivalent to an investment that went up 30%—and you can come out ahead even if the stock price goes down, provided it doesn't fall too far.

Yet it makes sense to do a projection (or have a tax pro do one) to find out how much AMT credit you can recover when you sell the shares. If you hold so many shares that you end up with a large unrecovered credit, you're taking added risk without any compensating tax benefit. If your ISO has a huge bargain element, there's no tax reason to hold more than about 35% of the shares.

Chapter 44
ISO Strategies: Good, Bad and Ugly

If you plan to hold some or all of the shares after exercising an incentive stock option, you should consider the strategies discussed below.

Exercise Early in the Year

One of the key pieces of advice to people exercising incentive stock options: *exercise early in the year.* There are two ways this can help you.

First, if you've held the option at least a year before exercising it, then you'll have to hold the stock only a year and a day before it's mature. If you exercised early in the year, you can sell before the following April 15 and use the sale proceeds to pay the AMT you owe as a result of exercising the option. That means you won't have to come up with cash out of pocket (or sell stock in a disqualifying disposition) to pay the tax.

Second, and often more important, exercising early in the year gives you the longest possible lookback period for the bail-out strategy discussed next.

Bailing Out

In the year 2000, many people who followed the standard advice to exercise their incentive stock options early in the year found to their woe that they exercised just when the stock market (especially the market for tech stocks) was at its peak. Some of those who continued to hold shares beyond the end of the year ended up with AMT liability greater than the remaining value of their shares. Many others escaped the potential tax trap, though, by selling the shares before the end of the year.

Example: You exercised an incentive stock option with $1,000,000 of profit early in the year. Toward the end of the year the stock is worth $200,000. If you continue to hold the stock, you'll owe $280,000 in AMT—more than the value of your stock. If you sell before the end of the year, you still have a profit of $200,000 and your tax is at most about 35% of that amount, leaving you $130,000 ahead instead of $80,000 in the hole.

Your situation doesn't have to be that extreme for a bail-out to make sense. Any time the stock value has declined enough so that the regular tax you'll pay on a current sale is less than the AMT you'll owe if you continue to hold the shares, you should consider selling at least some of them as a hedge against a further decline in value.

Example: You paid $20,000 to exercise an incentive stock option for $100,000 worth of stock. Later that year the stock is worth $70,000. If you continue to hold the stock, your AMT will be $25,000. (This is more than 28% because some of the income fell in the range where your AMT exemption amount is phased out.) If you sell the stock now, you'll pay less than $18,000 in regular income tax. There's limited tax advantage in continuing to hold the stock, and risk that you'll find trouble if the stock declines further after the end of the year and before you can sell it. You should seriously consider selling at least some of the stock now to moderate your risk.

When planning for the possibility of bailing out, keep in mind the possibility that you'll be unable to sell shares during some periods. If you're subject to rules that prevent you from selling around the time the company issues its financial reports, be sure to know those rules. Likewise, consider any lockup period or Rule 144 restriction that might prevent you from selling shares. Leave a margin for error, because it isn't always possible to sell shares on the date you're planning a sale.

Bad Bail-Outs

Many realize they need to do something about their AMT problem when their shares decline in value but don't know what action to take. As indicated above, simply selling your stock through a broker will do the trick (assuming that alternative is available). Here are some things that *don't* work:

- **Giving your stock to a family member.** This is a disqualifying disposition, but because it is not a sale, you're required to report as ordinary income (compensation) the entire spread as of the date you exercised the option, not the smaller profit that existed as of the time of the gift. Actually, it doesn't matter whether your donee is a family member: any gift creates this problem.

- **Giving the stock to charity.** It may seem as if this should bail you out of your bad situation, but it can actually make matters worse. Once again you have a disqualifying disposition and you have to report the original option spread as compensation income. You also get a charitable contribution deduction, but this deduction is limited to the current value of the stock. For example, if you paid $30,000 for stock worth $150,000 and later that year gave it to charity when it was worth $10,000, you would end up paying tax on $130,000 (the original spread of $140,000 reduced by the $10,000 charitable contribution deduction). That's certainly not the kind of tax relief you had in mind when you made this charitable donation. Selling the stock would eliminate the AMT altogether and allow you to deduct a capital loss. If you're charitably inclined, you can donate the cash proceeds *after* you sell the shares.

- **Selling your stock to a family member.** If you can't give the stock away, can you sell it to a family member? Sure, if you don't mind paying higher taxes. Once again, you're required to report the full spread from the time you exercised the option as compensation income.

- **Selling the stock and buying it back.** The rule here is the same as selling to a relative: if you buy the stock back within the "wash sale period" (which extends 30 days before and after the date of sale), you have to report the full spread from the date of exercise as compensation income. That's true even if you don't have a loss on the sale (the normal situation where the wash sale rule applies). A special rule says you're stuck paying the extra tax if your transaction even looks like a wash sale. Buying the stock back is likely to be a bad idea in any event—it's usually better to diversify—but if you feel this is the way you want to go, make sure you wait at least 31 days after your sale before buying replacement shares.

Year-End Mini-Exercise

If you're near the end of the year and thinking of exercising incentive stock options early the next year, consider exercising at least a small portion of your options before the end of the current year. The reason? In most situations you can exercise at least some options without incurring AMT. How much you can exercise with zero AMT depends on your situation. It can range from zero to tens of thousands of dollars. You'll have to do a calculation based on projected income and deduction figures to learn how big a freebie you can grab.

Eliminating AMT

Here's an idea that seems to make sense to lots of people, including some professional planners, but may not stand up to close scrutiny. You can eliminate AMT altogether on your incentive stock options if you use the "sell strategy" for some options and the "hold strategy" for others. If you work the numbers right, you won't pay any additional tax in the year you exercised your incentive stock options. Yet there's a hidden cost to this strategy.

> **Example:** Your income for the current year is $75,000 and your tax would be $14,500 if you didn't exercise any options. You decide to exercise incentive stock options that have a bargain element of $100,000. If you choose to hold all the shares until the end of the year, you'll owe $25,500 in AMT for total federal tax of $40,000. Spending some time with a calculator, you find that you can pay the same tax if you sell shares with $83,000 of profit and hold shares with $17,000 of profit. Your tax isn't any higher or lower, but now you're paying $40,000 of regular income tax and no AMT.

To many people this looks like a great idea. You avoided AMT, and you didn't pay any additional tax. The trouble is, you *will* pay additional tax the *following* year.

Here's why. If you held additional shares, incurring some AMT in the year you exercised the option, you would qualify for an AMT credit in the year of sale. When you sell enough shares to eliminate AMT completely, you eliminate the AMT credit as well. You have to look ahead to your likely tax situation in the year *after* you exercise an incentive stock option to get the complete picture of how these transactions will affect your taxes.

It can certainly make sense to sell shares to *reduce* the amount of AMT you pay in the year of exercise. That's a good way to moderate the amount of risk you bear from holding shares in your company's stock. What's more, as the previous chapter discusses, after a certain point your only benefit from holding additional shares is building up an unused AMT credit.

Yet many ISO holders will find that they give up too much of the tax benefit if they arrange to sell enough shares to completely eliminate AMT. That's especially true after the reduction in income tax rates in recent years. The highest tax rates are now so close to the highest income tax rates that you may find the only way to eliminate AMT completely is to sell almost all your ISO shares the same year you exercise the option.

Eliminating Excess AMT Credit

In some situations, especially when you have extremely valuable stock options, you may be able to project that you will end up with unused AMT credit after you sell your stock. A more sophisticated (and less costly) version of the strategy discussed above would be to sell just enough shares to eliminate the *excess* AMT credit: the credit that would otherwise be unused. Before adopting this approach, you should consider your ability to use the excess AMT credit in subsequent years. Even after you've sold all your ISO stock, you can continue to recover AMT credit that resulted from exercise of the incentive stock option. Having an AMT credit carryover isn't an indication of bad tax planning if it's small enough so you can expect to use it in the reasonably foreseeable future.

If your situation is such that you expect to have more AMT credit than you can use within a few years, it certainly makes sense to sell some of your ISO stock at the time of exercise. There's little or no tax benefit when you hold more shares, and you can reduce your investment risk by selling some now. Even if you believe you may use up the AMT credit eventually, the delay in using the credit means its *present value* is smaller than the dollar amount of the credit would indicate. In short, it may make sense to sell some of your ISO stock to reduce or eliminate the excess credit you'll have after selling the shares. This is a strategy to reduce investment risk at relatively little (but not necessarily zero) tax cost.

State Taxes

There are two important reasons to think about state income tax when you plan for the exercise of incentive stock options. The first is that some states have their own alternative minimum tax. If you live in California, for example, you can expect to pay a hefty amount of state

AMT on top of federal AMT when you exercise an incentive stock option.

You also need to think about state taxes as they affect your federal AMT. State taxes are deductible if you itemize, but the deduction isn't allowed for AMT purposes. Proper timing of the payment of state taxes can reduce the amount of AMT you pay, or increase the amount of AMT that qualifies for the AMT credit. You may not have a lot of control over when you pay your state income taxes, but to the extent you have a choice you may save money if you time those payments for maximum advantage in connection with the federal AMT.

Chapter 45
Using Tax Carryovers

Many planning mistakes relate to a misunderstanding of the appropriate use of tax carryovers. It isn't just amateurs that make these errors. Tax pros and financial planners make these miscues all too often, and on occasion they crop up in planning tips that appear in the financial press. I suspect they stem from an erroneous application of the principle of time value of money.

Time Value of Money

The time value of money is an intuitive concept, and an important one in financial planning. The basic idea is that a dollar you hold today is worth more than a dollar you will receive at some point in the future. It's easy to see this if you consider that you can invest the current dollar in a risk-free interest-bearing account and have *more than* a dollar at the time when you are to receive the future dollar.

For present purposes we don't have to get into the details of present value discounting of future cash flows. The main point is that the time value of money plays an important role in tax planning. Generally speaking, you're better off if you can delay a tax payment without increasing it. A huge amount of tax planning revolves around the idea of delaying tax payments. Examples include the use of 401k plans and IRAs, accelerated depreciation for business equipment, and timing of stock sales and other securities transactions.

The flip side is also important: when you have money coming back from the IRS, it's better to get it sooner. Even if you don't plan to invest your refund, you probably want to receive it ASAP. That's a valid concept, but the springboard for many mistakes in handling tax carryovers.

Tax Carryovers

We're using the term *tax carryovers* to refer to any benefit you can use in a later year if you don't fully use it this year. One that you may run into while handling your stock options is the *capital loss carryover*. When you have capital losses in excess of capital gains, you can use only $3,000 of the excess as a deduction against your ordinary income. The rest of the capital loss carries over to the following year.

If you have incentive stock options, you may run into a different kind of carryover. In the year you exercise your options you're likely to pay alternative minimum tax if you decide to hold the shares. In the following year you may be entitled to an *AMT credit.* Any portion of the credit you don't recover in the year after you paid AMT carries over to the following year.

It's worth noting that both of these items carry over *indefinitely.* If you don't use them up in the second year they carry to the third year and so on. Under normal circumstances there's no particular urgency to use them right away.

Where Planning Goes Wrong

A carryover is a tax benefit you haven't used yet. It seems to make sense that you're better off if you use it sooner. Why let the IRS continue to hold your money? This is the thought process that leads to much erroneous planning.

> **Example:** You have a $10,000 capital loss and, so far, no capital gains. If you do nothing, you'll deduct $3,000 and have a $7,000 capital loss carryover. Fortunately, you have an investment with a built-in gain of $7,000. To avoid delaying the use of your capital loss, you sell the investment and buy another investment (or perhaps buy the same one back again).

Chances are you just shot yourself in the foot. This maneuver didn't recover any cash from the IRS. You "recovered" the benefit by increasing your capital gain income. You didn't use the capital loss to reduce your taxes—you used taxes to reduce your capital loss.

In this example you didn't pay any additional tax in the year these events occurred. What about the following year? If you hadn't burned up your capital loss, you would have a carryover you could use in the second year to offset capital gains. Even if you had no capital gains in the second year, you could have used $3,000 of the capital loss to reduce your taxes and carried the remaining $4,000 to the following year. That opportunity went down the drain when you went out of your way to create a capital gain in the first year.

What you really did was convert one tax benefit—the capital loss—into another one: higher basis for whatever investment you used to replace the one that had the $7,000 gain. You may recover the benefit of the higher basis when you sell the replacement asset. What did you gain in the meantime? Nothing at all. You may have been hurt by using the capital loss against a long-term capital gain instead of using it against short-term gain or up to $3,000 of ordinary income. You may have been hurt further by delay in the use of the benefit while it's "locked up" as part of the basis of the replacement investment. Meanwhile you incurred unnecessary transaction costs as part of the planning that put you in this unfavorable position.

AMT Credit

Some planners who are sophisticated enough to avoid the mistake in the example above plunge into even worse mistakes in dealing with the AMT credit.

> **Example:** You exercised an incentive stock option the previous year and sold the stock this year. Preliminary calculations indicate you won't make full use of your AMT credit this year despite selling all the stock. Your financial advisor points out that

you can recover more of the credit if you exercise some nonqualified stock options. The added income will be taxed at about 35% under the regular tax and 28% under the AMT, so increasing your income by $100,000 will allow you to claim about $7,000 more of your AMT credit.

Let's assume for the moment that you don't have independent reasons for wanting to exercise the nonqualified stock options. The only reason you're considering this maneuver is to recover more of your AMT credit. Does this make sense?

Absolutely not! This maneuver is even worse than burning a capital loss, because it involves *increasing* your tax in the year you exercise the nonqualified stock options. Planners sometimes seem to think the benefit of "recovering" the AMT credit outweighs the detriment of paying tax sooner than necessary on the nonqualified stock options. Yet you didn't really *recover* anything. You *burned up* some or all of your remaining AMT credit, which would have been just as valuable in a later year. What's worse, your planning caused you to pay additional tax in the year you exercised the nonqualified stock options. Once again, you used taxes to reduce a tax benefit, instead of using a tax benefit to reduce taxes.

> ▪ Think twice before adopting a strategy designed to accelerate your ability to use a tax carryover.

Chapter 46
Private or Pre-IPO Companies

Much of our discussion has proceeded with the implicit or explicit assumption that your company's stock is publicly traded. Some companies prefer to remain privately held, while others intend to be publicly traded but are not yet ready for their initial public offering, or IPO. These companies are subject to the same tax rules that apply publicly traded companies, but some of the planning considerations may be different.

Value of the Stock

The value of publicly traded stock is generally the current price established by the stock market. Without this objective measure, we need another way to determine the value of stock in private companies. In most cases where a private company issues options, the board of directors (or a committee of the board) announces the value from time to time.

The most persuasive factor in valuing privately held stock is the price paid in recent arms-length sales. Yet pre-IPO companies often sell stock to venture capitalists and other investors under special terms that provide the purchaser with rights beyond those of ordinary shareholders. The "VCs" may receive preferred stock, or special voting rights, or representation on the board of directors, or all of the above. As a result, the price they pay for their shares may bear little relationship to the value of shares you can buy with your stock options. It isn't unusual for the announced price of common shares to be a small fraction of the price paid by venture capitalists in a recent round of financing.

The value of your company can depend on a variety of other factors, such as profits, cash flow, or net worth (assets minus debts and other liabilities). In some industries the value of a company may relate closely to a particular measure, such as the number and size of accounts or how many people visit the company's web site. Inevitably the value of a private company is somewhat subjective.

Value of Your Option

If the value of the stock is somewhat subjective, the value of your options is even more so. The Black-Scholes formula is useless without an indication of the stock's volatility. If the stock isn't publicly traded, we have no way of telling how much the value of the stock fluctuates from time to time.

In most situations it's appropriate to treat pre-IPO stock as if it were highly volatile.* That means the time value of the option may be unusually high. It also means there's a significant chance that you'll never reap any value at all from your option. Very often, options on pre-IPO stock are like lottery tickets, paying off at very high levels or not paying off at all.

High-Risk Stock Compensation

A consultant I spoke with received close to $500,000 worth of pre-IPO stock for his services. He hoped the stock would be worth millions after the IPO, but the company failed to go public and the stock ended up being worthless. Because the stock was worth $500,000 when he received it, he owed about $200,000 of income tax and self-employment tax. This is a case where someone took a huge risk even though he paid nothing at all for the stock.

Proper planning would have allowed him to avoid this situation. For example, instead of $500,000 worth of stock

---

* For some purposes the IRS will value an option on a privately held company by comparison to options on a comparable public company.

he could have accepted options worth $500,000. Delayed vesting is another approach that might work in a situation like this. Because of the risk the stock would be worthless, it was important to avoid owing tax now on its speculative value.

High-Risk Option Exercise

When you exercise an option on pre-IPO stock, you take economic risk in addition to tax risk. No matter how good the company's prospects seem, there's no way to be sure an IPO will be successful until it actually happens. When you exercise an option prior to an IPO you should take into account the very real possibility that your stock will turn out to be worthless. In that event you can be stuck with the tax consequences of exercising the option and the loss of any funds used to exercise the option.

Compare those risks with the potential payoff from exercising your option before the IPO. On a pre-tax basis you're in the same position either way. There may be a significant tax benefit in exercising earlier, however.

> **Example:** You have an option to buy 10,000 shares of pre-IPO stock at $1 per share. The current value of the stock is $2 per share. You believe a successful IPO is likely, and will leave you with stock worth $20 per share. If you exercise the option after the IPO, you'll have to report $190,000 of compensation income (the $200,000 value reduced by the $10,000 purchase price). Your after-tax profit is about $124,000.
>
> If instead you exercise the option now, you'll report only $10,000 of compensation income. Later you'll report $180,000 of long-term capital gain on a sale of the stock for $200,000. Your after-tax profit goes up by $36,000, because you converted $180,000 from compensation income (taxed at an assumed rate of 35%) to long-term capital gain (taxed at 15%).

Well, $36,000 is a nice chunk of change, but you're taking a lot more risk to get there. If the IPO doesn't come off, your stock may turn out to be worthless. You'll have lost the $10,000 you paid to exercise the option plus another $3,500 or so you have to pay on the compensation income you report when you exercise the option. You'll also have a potential tax benefit from a $20,000 capital loss on the sale or worthlessness of your shares, but you may not get full benefit for that loss because of the $3,000 capital loss limitation.

Part XII
Other Topics

This part of the book covers topics you may need to understand when dealing with compensation in stock and options, even though they don't fit in the previous categories.

Part X
Other Topics

Chapter 47
Fair Market Value

When you report compensation income from stock or options, the amount of income will be measured by the *fair market value* of the stock. There's a classical definition of this term that many tax professionals know by heart:

> Fair market value is the price at which the property would change hands between a willing buyer and a willing seller, neither being under any compulsion to buy or to sell and both having reasonable knowledge of relevant facts.

This definition takes you a good part of the way toward understanding the concept. To complete the picture we'll discuss the following topics:

- Valuing publicly traded stock

- Valuing privately held stock

- How restrictions affect value

- Discounts

Valuing Publicly Traded Stock

Stock is publicly traded if you can buy or sell it on an established securities market, or through some other system that acts as the equivalent of a securities market. In general the stock market determines the value of publicly traded stock. The usual rule is that the value on any given day is the average of the high and low selling prices on that day.

Employers sometimes use variations on this rule. If the stock is very thinly traded, it may make sense to use an average over a period of several trading days so that a single transaction won't have undue effect on the value. There isn't any regulation that permits this approach, but we don't see the IRS challenging reasonable variations unless they provide opportunities for manipulation.

It's somewhat unusual, but not impossible, for publicly traded stock to qualify for a blockage discount as explained below.

Valuing Privately Held Stock

If your stock isn't publicly traded as explained above, it's *privately held*. A full discussion of valuation for privately held stock is beyond our scope—there are entire books written on the subject. Here are some of the main points:

- **Recent transactions.** The strongest indication of the value of stock on a given date is an actual arm's length sale occurring near that date. A sale is at *arm's length* if there isn't any family or other relationship between the buyer and seller that might lead to a sale at a price different than fair market value. If you want to claim that your stock has a value of $10 per share, you'll have a hard time supporting that claim if someone recently paid $50 per share.*

- **Other valuation methods.** Sometimes there are no recent sales that can be used to establish the value of stock. Then you have to estimate the value of the entire company and divide by the number of shares outstanding to find the value per share.

---

* Venture capitalists making a major investment in a company often receive preferred shares or other consideration (such as board representation or warrants) that affect the amount they pay for their shares. In this type of situation it may be reasonable to price the shares you receive as compensation considerably lower than the per-share price of the financing deal.

Different types of methods are appropriate for different types of businesses. Most focus in some way on profits (or an element of revenues that should be indicative of profit potential), but the value of the company's assets may come into play also. The *book value* of a company (the value of its assets minus its liabilities, as shown on the company's financial records) is sometimes seen as a *minimum* value the company must have, but some companies have a value that far exceeds book value. Inevitably there's an element of subjectivity in determining the fair market value of a closely held business.

> ▪ Because value is somewhat subjective, taxpayers frequently find themselves in court with the IRS over valuation issues. Yet few of these cases involve the value of shares used as compensation, mainly because there are two sides to the issue: a lower value may reduce your income tax, but also gives the company a smaller deduction.

Effect of Restrictions

You may feel that restrictions on the stock you acquired make it less valuable than it would otherwise be. But there's a special rule here: when you determine the value of your shares, you have to ignore all restrictions except those that are permanent. If your stock is restricted for a limited period of time, or until some event occurs, you have to ignore the restriction when you determine the value of the stock.

Certain permanent restrictions count in determining value, however. The tax law refers to these as *non-lapse restrictions*. If your stock is subject to a permanent restriction, you may be able to take that restriction into account in determining the value of the stock. See Chapter 31 for details.

Discounts

There are circumstances that can justify a discount in the value of your stock. One recognized discount applies when there's no market for the stock: a discount for *lack of marketability*. Another discount can apply where there's a market for the stock, but the size of your holdings is large enough to make efficient sale impossible: a *blockage* discount. The availability of these discounts, and the appropriate size of the discount, should be determined by a qualified appraiser or tax professional.

Chapter 48
Compensation Income

This book refers often to *compensation income*. Of course you're familiar with compensation income in general, going back to the first time you received a paycheck. There are two special considerations connected with equity compensation, though. First, withholding is required for certain forms of equity compensation provided to employees. When the compensation takes the form of stock, special arrangements are necessary to satisfy the withholding requirement. And second, if you're not an employee, you need to be aware of not only your income tax liability but also your obligations under the self-employment tax.

Withholding for Employees Only

Most types of equity compensation may be received by non-employees (such as directors or consultants) as well as employees. Withholding is required only for employees (and, in some cases, former employees). Note that if you aren't an employee you'll generally have to pay self-employment tax on any amount that's treated as compensation.

When Withholding Is Required

In general, withholding is required in situations where an employee is required to report compensation income:

- Withholding is required when you receive a grant of vested stock (or make the section 83b election for unvested stock).

- Withholding is required when your previously unvested stock vests (assuming you didn't make the section 83b election).

- Withholding is required when you exercise a nonqualified option.

There's an exception to this general rule. If you have compensation income from disposing of stock acquired by exercising an incentive stock option or through an employee stock purchase plan, the IRS doesn't require withholding.

How to Meet the Withholding Requirement

The special problem in withholding on compensation paid in stock is that you aren't receiving any money. Naturally the IRS insists that the withholding be provided in cash. How can you provide cash withholding when you didn't receive any money?

Some companies help with this problem by providing some form of cash compensation that goes along with the stock. This may take the form of a stock appreciation right or cash bonus plan. Note, however, if the company covers your withholding, the amount they pay for that purpose is *additional* taxable income to you.

> **Example:** You receive stock valued at $20,000 and the withholding obligation is $5,000. If the company covers this withholding for you, then you have another $5,000 of compensation income (and the company has to withhold on *that*). The company would have to provide about $6,700 to cover all the bases at this rate of withholding. (This is called *grossing up* the payment.)

Most companies expect *you* to cover the withholding. That means you have to come up with the cash and pay it to the company, which in turn pays it to the IRS. You may have to withdraw that amount from savings, or perhaps even borrow to cover the payment. It may be possible to use the stock you're receiving as security for the loan.

One approach is to sell some or all of the stock that was provided as compensation, and use the sale proceeds to meet the withholding requirement. The company may agree to buy back some of the stock, or arrange for it to be sold by a broker, for example. In these cases you need to consider the tax effects of the sale as well as the receipt of the stock.

Consequences of Withholding

Regardless of how you satisfy the requirement, the income tax withholding will be a credit on your income tax return. It will reduce the amount of tax due or increase the amount of your refund.

Don't make the mistake of thinking the withholding is part of your cost for the stock. You can't include the withholding in the basis of the stock you received, even though it was an amount you had to pay to the company when you received it.

You should be aware that the amount of withholding on this compensation may or may not be enough to cover the amount of tax that will actually result. Withholding formulas don't precisely match the tax liability. It pays to do a calculation of the actual amount of tax you'll owe with respect to this compensation to avoid an unpleasant surprise on April 15.

Social Security and Self-Employment Tax

Social security and self-employment tax walk hand-in-hand. The first applies to employees, and the second applies to everyone else. When you're an employee, you pay half of the social security tax through withholding, and your employer pays the other half. (The half that's paid by your employer doesn't show up on your pay stub, so many people aren't aware that the employer pays "matching dollars" for the social security tax that's withheld from their pay.) If you provide services but you're not an employee, you're *self-employed*. The tax law treats you as if you were both the employer and the employee, and that means you have to pay both halves of the tax on your net earnings from self-employment.

Whether or not you're an employee, these taxes apply only to the portion of your income that counts as compensation. Whenever this book describes an element of income as *compensation income*, you can plan on being hit with one of these taxes. (There's an exception for early disposition of stock from an incentive stock option or disposition of ESPP stock.) Any income described as *capital gain* is exempt from social security tax and self-employment tax. The same is true for other investment income, such as interest and dividends (except dividends on stock that isn't vested).

Two components of the tax. The social security tax and self-employment tax are made up of two components. One component is for hospital insurance (HI), and the other covers all other programs under social security: old age, survivors and disability insurance (OASDI). There's an income limit on the OASDI portion, known as the *wage base*. There's no income limit on the HI portion. If you earn enough income as an employee to exceed the wage base, you'll have the pleasant experience of seeing your paycheck suddenly become larger at the point in the year when OASDI withholding drops out. You'll continue paying the lower HI rate, however.

The wage base is the same for both social security and self-employment tax. It's adjusted each year for inflation. For 2004 the amount is $87,900. Up to that amount, an employee pays social security tax at the rate of 7.65%, which consists of a 6.2% OASDI tax and 1.45% HI tax. Above that amount, only the 1.45% HI tax applies. All along the way, the employer is paying the same amount, too. If you're self-employed, your self-employment tax is basically double that amount, at an overall rate of 15.3% up to the wage base and 2.9% above that amount. There's a technical adjustment in these rates to give you the benefit of the deduction you would receive on the employer portion of the tax if you were actually paying wages to an employee, instead of "employing" yourself.

Finally, there are some people who have wages as an employee and also have self-employment income in the same year. In this situation, you'll get a break on the self-employment tax if your total compensation income is above the wage base. You'll pay the higher rate only on the portion of the wage base that wasn't taken up by your earnings as an employee.

Example: In 2004, you earn $60,000 as an employee and also have $40,000 of net earnings from self-employment. All of the $60,000, and the first $27,900 of self-employment earnings, will be subject to the higher rate that includes OASDI. The rest of the self-employment earnings will be subject only to the lower HI tax, because it's above the $87,900 wage base.

Chapter 49
Estimated Tax Payments

If you're an employee, you may have never had to worry about making estimated tax payments. The amount of income tax withheld from paychecks may be enough to cover the tax you owe and then some, providing a refund. Even if you owe some tax on April 15, estimates aren't required unless you owe more than $1,000.

When you receive compensation in stock and options, there's a good chance you'll end up with a tax bill of more than $1,000 at some point. In that situation, it's possible that you'll incur a penalty if you don't make quarterly payments of estimated tax.

First Things You Should Know

If you've never had to deal with estimated taxes before, the whole idea can seem foreign and uncomfortable. There are two things you should know right away to put your mind at rest.

- **It's easy.** In most cases, the process of figuring out how much to pay isn't hard at all. And paying the tax is a snap.

- **No jail time.** You won't go to jail if you make a mistake and pay too little. In fact, the penalty isn't exactly a killer. It's just simple interest on the amount you underpaid, and the interest rate isn't terribly high. If you somehow blow it and under-pay by $400, and correct the underpayment with your next payment three months later, your penalty might be about $10. It's better to avoid the penalty, but really, this is nothing to lose sleep over.

General Rule: 90%

The general rule is that your estimated tax payments, when added to your withholding and credits, must add up to 90% of the current year's tax liability. If your withholding and credits already add up to 90% of your tax liability, you don't have to make estimated tax payments. Yet in many cases you don't have to make estimated tax payments even if your withholding and credits fall short of the 90% figure, for reasons described below.

> ▪ When we talk about the *tax due*, we mean the total amount of tax you owe—including any self-employment tax and the dreaded alternative minimum tax (AMT).

Tax Due Less Than $1,000

Here's a rule that makes it easy for many people who have withholding that falls just a bit short to avoid dealing with estimated tax payments. No payment is required if the amount due after subtracting withholding and credits will be less than $1,000.

Example: Suppose you expect your wage withholding to be just enough to cover your income tax liability. Then you have a $4,000 long-term capital gain you didn't plan on. This gain will be taxed at 20%, so the added tax is $800. You can make an estimated tax payment if you feel more comfortable doing so, but there won't be a penalty if you wait until April 15 of next year to send in the payment because it's less than $1,000.

The only problem with this rule is that sometimes it's difficult to know what your tax liability will be. But $1,000 is a reasonable amount of leeway for the majority of taxpayers.

Prior Year Safe Harbor

Most people can avoid paying estimated tax if their withholding and credits equal 100% of the tax shown on the *prior year's* income tax return. I call this the *prior year safe harbor.*

There's a related rule. You don't have to pay estimated tax if all of the following are true:

- You had no tax liability for the previous year.

- You were a U.S. citizen or resident for the entire year.

- Your tax year covered a 12-month period.

This rule often permits taxpayers to avoid making estimated payments if they receive a large sum of income on a one-time basis.

> **Example:** In a normal year withholding is enough to cover your income tax—in fact, you usually get a small refund. In 2000 you exercise an incentive stock option and then sell the stock. As a result, you report $200,000 of income. Despite this huge increase in income, you don't have to make estimated tax payments if your withholding will be at least equal to the tax shown on the prior year's tax return.

> ▪ **Higher income, higher percentage.** There's a rule that requires taxpayers with adjusted gross income above $150,000 on the prior year's return ($75,000 if married filing separately) to pay 110% of the prior year's tax (not just 100%) when applying the prior year safe harbor. Congress has been known to tinker with this percentage, so check the form instructions.

Even if the prior year safe harbor doesn't allow you to completely avoid making estimated tax payments, it permits you to determine an amount that will avoid a penalty without making an accurate estimate of the current year's taxes.

Example: Your income tax for 2003 was $24,000. You expect your withholding for 2004 to be $21,000. You don't know how much income you'll have for 2004, though, because you may sell stock at a gain. Because of the prior year safe harbor, you can safely cover your estimated tax requirement by paying $3,000 ($750 per quarter). When added to your $21,000 of withholding, you'll have total payments that equal your prior year's tax.

There are situations where it doesn't make sense to use the prior year safe harbor. You may have a year in which you had an unusually large amount of income. When the next year rolls around, you would be paying estimates that are larger than necessary if you pay based on that banner year. In this case you'll want to estimate the current year's tax and try to pay at least 90% of that number.

Example: In 2003 you exercised nonqualified options and reported an extra $80,000 of income. In 2004 you won't have that extra income, but still need to make estimated tax payments. If you base the payment amount on your 2003 tax, you'll pay $30,000 more than necessary. It makes more sense to use a realistic estimate of your 2004 tax.

Estimating Your Tax

As you've seen above, there are plenty of situations where it isn't actually necessary to do any estimating when you make estimated tax payments. But sometimes you need to make an estimate of the current year's tax. Otherwise you'll either pay way too much, or come up short and end up with a penalty.

Form 1040-ES (the form used to pay estimated tax) comes with a worksheet you can use to estimate how much tax you'll owe for the current year. There's certainly nothing wrong with using this worksheet—but most people don't. The reason is that the worksheet takes you through more detail than may be necessary, but still leaves you with nothing better than an educated guess about your tax liability. You don't file the worksheet with the IRS, and there's no requirement to justify how you came up with the amount of your estimated tax payment. So most people use a somewhat simplified method to figure their estimated tax:

- Look at each number on the prior year's tax return and ask yourself if this year's number is likely to be significantly different. Ignore differences in wages because there will be a corresponding difference in withholding. Use rounded numbers and don't worry about minor changes.

- Add up all the differences to see how much larger or smaller your taxable income will be for the current year.

- Apply the tax rates to see how much difference this will make in your income tax. (If the difference results from a long-term capital gain, apply the capital gain tax rates.) Round the number up or simply tack on an added amount if you want to increase your comfort level about avoiding a penalty.

Many people using this method don't bother looking up the changes in the tax rates that result from inflation adjustments. These changes will decrease your tax slightly, so that's one way of providing a cushion of extra payments.

Voluntary Payments

Depending on your situation, the amount of estimated tax you're *required* to pay could be quite a bit less than your true estimate of the amount of tax you'll owe. That's because you're allowed to pay estimates based on the previous year's tax, even if you know this year's tax will be higher. When that happens you have a choice. You can pay the minimum amount required—and pay the rest on April 15. Or you can pay something close to the true estimate so you won't owe a lot on April 15. Which is better depends on your comfort level and money management skills.

Pay now and relax. Some people choose to make estimated payments even when the payments aren't required. The reason? Perhaps they're concerned that the money won't be there when they need it to pay taxes. Perhaps they're simply more comfortable knowing that they won't have a huge tax bill in April. There are a variety of good reasons to make estimated tax payments even if the payments aren't legally required. The biggest one is peace of mind.

Pay later and earn. The main reason *not* to pay more than you have to is that you lose the use of your money between the time you pay the estimate and the time you would have sent payment with your return. You should be able to earn at least a little bit of interest during that time. So there's at least one good reason to pay later, even though there are good reasons to pay sooner.

> ▪ If you take this approach, *don't get greedy*. Money you need for a tax payment next April should be invested conservatively to eliminate risk of loss.

Which is better. Which approach is better—making voluntary payments, or paying the minimum—depends on your personality and your circumstances. Consider the following example:

Example: You normally don't pay estimates because your income is mainly from wages subject to withholding. In January 2004 you sell stock and have a capital gain of $30,000. You expect to owe $6,000 of tax, but you don't have to pay estimates because your 2004 withholding will be at least equal to your 2003 tax.

You have several choices, including the following:

- You can put $6,000 aside in an interest bearing account until April 15, 2005 when the tax is due. This way you can make a little profit on the money before sending it to the IRS. If you have the discipline to leave the money alone, you come out ahead using this approach. There's a danger, though. If you start with this intention, but end up spending the money on a trip to Aruba, or losing it in a high-risk investment, you may wake up with a headache on April 15, 2005.

- You can send in a single estimated payment of $6,000. This approach is easy, and may seem relatively painless if you do it at a time when you're flush with money from the stock sale. It's also very safe: this approach assures that you won't somehow lose or spend the money before you file your tax return. It doesn't allow you to earn interest on the $6,000, though.

- You can send in four quarterly estimates of $1,500 each. You may prefer this approach if you don't like the idea of writing a single check for $6,000 to the IRS (who does?). And this approach gives you the flexibility to reduce later payments if you have a capital loss or other reduction in taxable income later in the year. There's a little more paperwork involved in this approach though, and more opportunity to lose or spend the money before you file your return.

There's nothing illegal or immoral about any of these approaches. They're all equally acceptable to the IRS. (They won't be upset if they receive a $6,000 payment for one quarter and no payment in later quarters.) If you find yourself in a situation like this, choose the approach that works best for you.

Increasing Your Withholding

There's a way you may be able to cover your extra tax liability without making estimated tax payments: increase the amount of tax withheld from your paycheck. You get a special benefit with this approach: extra withholding that comes late in the year is treated the same as if it was spread evenly over the year. You can use this approach to avoid late payment penalties.

How to do it. To increase the amount of federal income tax withheld from your paycheck, ask your employer for a new Form W-4. You're required to fill out this form when you start working for an employer. You can fill out a new one whenever your circumstances call for a change in the amount of withholding.

This form contains several worksheets, and the instructions tell you to "complete all worksheets that apply." But the worksheets are there mainly to make sure you don't *reduce* your withholding more than you're supposed to. There's never a problem when you want to *increase* your withholding. You can fill out the worksheets if you want, but you're not required to do so. And there's no particular need if the only thing you're doing is increasing your withholding to cover tax on your equity compensation.

There are two ways to increase your withholding on this form. One is to reduce the number of allowances you claim on the form. This can be a little tricky, because you don't necessarily know how much your withholding will change when you change your allowances. The amount depends on your income level and the withholding method adopted by your employer.

> ▪ Some people are confused by *allowances*. You get one allowance for each exemption you can claim on your tax return (yourself, your spouse and your dependents), but an allowance isn't the same as an exemption. There are allowances for other items, such as deductions and certain credits. Reducing your allowances doesn't mean you'll claim fewer exemptions when you file your tax return. The number of allowances is used *only* to determine how much tax is withheld from your paycheck.

There's another approach that's simpler: request an "additional amount" to be withheld from your paycheck. Do this on line 6 of the form. This makes it fairly easy to determine the amount of the increase when you file Form W-4.

Check with your employer to find out when the change will go into effect. Normally there's a time lag between the day you fill out this form and the day it's processed, so you may not see the change in your very next paycheck. Keep an eye on your paycheck stubs to confirm that the change was properly made, and had the effect you anticipated.

Avoiding late payment penalty. The nice thing about using withholding to cover your estimated tax liability is that it can get you out of a late payment penalty. Withholding is presumed to be received evenly throughout the year.

> **Example:** Suppose you realize in May that you need to pay $6,000 estimated tax for the year, and you've already blown the first $1,500 payment that was due April 15. It won't be a big deal if you send in the payment a few weeks late because the penalty isn't all that terrible. But you can avoid the penalty altogether by increasing your withholding for the rest of the year by $6,000. The IRS will assume the withholding occurred evenly throughout the year, with $1,500 coming in the first quarter. You get the benefit of this assumption even if all of the added withholding comes in December!

Making Estimated Payments

Estimated payments for any year are due on April 15, June 15 and September 15 of that year, and January 15 of the following year. Whenever one of these dates falls on a legal holiday or on a weekend, the due date is the next day that isn't a holiday or weekend day. Here are some points to keep in mind:

- If you owe money with your tax return, *and* have to make an estimated tax payment, you have *two* checks to write on April 15. Be prepared!

- Although the payments are "quarterly," they aren't three months apart. The second payment sneaks up on you, just two months after the first one.

- Like your tax return, estimated payments are considered "on time" if you *mail* them by the due date.

- Most states that have an income tax require estimated payments on the same schedule as the federal payments. If you itemize deductions, it may be to your advantage to make your fourth quarter state estimated tax payment in December, not January, so you can deduct it a year earlier.

- A small number of individual taxpayers use a fiscal tax year that ends with a month other than December. Their payment schedule is different (but equivalent): the fifteenth day of the fourth, sixth and ninth months of their fiscal year, and the fifteenth day of the first month of the following fiscal year.

What to file. When you make estimated tax payments you need to enclose Form 1040-ES, Estimated Tax Voucher. This form is about as simple as they get. It asks for your name, address and social security number—and just one other item: the amount you're paying.

If you've previously made estimated tax payments, the IRS will send forms with your name, address and social security number pre-printed. Even if this is your first year paying estimates, the IRS will send pre-printed forms after they receive your first payment. You're not *required* to use these forms—don't panic if you lose them—but the IRS *prefers* that you use them to help assure that your payment will be processed promptly and correctly.

Form 1040-ES comes from the IRS as part of an intimidating package that includes lengthy instructions and detailed worksheets. As mentioned earlier, you don't have to fill out the worksheets unless you think they'll be helpful. And you should *never* send these worksheets to the IRS.

Other important tips. *Estimated tax payments don't go to the same address as your return!* Don't enclose an estimated tax payment with your Form 1040. Check the instructions for Form 1040-ES for the proper address.

Enclose your check. Write your social security number on the check and a notation of what it's for, like this: 2004 2Q Form 1040-ES (assuming it's for the second quarter of 2004). If you're doing this before your first cup of coffee in the morning, double check to see that you *signed* the check.

You don't have to justify your estimated tax payments. In fact, there's no place for a *signature* on the form. When you send it in, you're not promising that this is the correct amount. All you're saying is, "Here's a payment to be applied toward my taxes."

Be sure to keep an accurate record of your estimated tax payments so you can claim credit for them when you file your return.

Joint payments. If you're married, you can make joint estimated tax payments with your spouse. (There's an exception if either spouse is a nonresident alien.) Paying joint estimated payments does *not* mean you have to file a joint return. But if you end up filing separately, you'll have to sort out who gets credit for what amount.

Chapter 50
Identifying Shares

If you find yourself holding different batches of shares in the same company, you may want to be able to choose which shares you sell first. That's especially true when dealing with equity compensation. Selling the wrong shares can be disastrous.

> **Example:** You hold some shares of stock you bought on the open market, and also some shares of stock from exercising an incentive stock option. You intend to sell the shares you bought on the open market. If you make a mistake and sell the shares from the incentive stock option, you may have a disqualifying disposition and be required to report compensation income.

The rules for identifying shares aren't difficult, but are often misunderstood. Many brokers are confused by them. Make sure *you* understand them, so your broker's ignorance won't cost you tax dollars.

Background

It's useful to understand the *theory* of the rule before you understand the rule. The tax law permits you to decide what shares you want to sell. But you have to make that choice *at the time of the sale*. You can't go back later, after you see how things turn out for the year, and say you really meant to sell different shares. The rules for identifying shares are designed to do two things:

- Provide a rule for what happens if you didn't make any choice at the time of the sale, and

- Provide a way for you to make a choice at that time—and to prove that you made it.

If You Don't Choose

If you don't specify which shares you're selling, the law treats you as if you sold the *earliest* shares you bought. This is called the *first-in, first out* method, or *FIFO*.

> **Example:** You bought 50 shares of XYZ at $40 in 1997 and another 50 at $60 in 1998. In 2004 you sell 50 shares at $80 without specifying which shares you're selling. The tax law says you sold the shares you bought in 1997.

Notice that you would report a smaller gain, and pay less tax, if you specified that you were selling the shares you bought in 1998. Sometimes it pays to choose which shares you're selling.

No averaging. Some people wonder if they can use the *average* basis for the shares they hold. There are averaging rules for mutual fund shares, but for regular stocks you can't use average basis.

Switching permitted. Suppose you sold some shares earlier and didn't identify the shares you were selling. Does this mean you're locked into using the first-in, first-out method? Not at all. The rule for identifying stock applies to each individual sale. You can identify shares for a current sale even if you failed to identify shares from the same stock in the past. (Note, however, that if you elect averaging for mutual fund shares you're locked into that method for all shares of the same mutual fund.)

If You Hold Certificates

Shares of stock are represented by *certificates*. It used to be commonplace (and is still not unusual) for shareholders to hold certificates for their shares. Most investors nowadays leave the certificates with the broker.

If you hold certificates for your shares, the way you choose which shares you're selling is to deliver the certificate that represents those shares. It isn't necessary to *identify* the shares in this situation. It's your responsibility to determine which certificate represents the shares you want to sell and deliver that certificate. It won't help to tell the broker (or the IRS) you meant to sell some other shares if you deliver the wrong certificate.

It's possible you'll end up holding a single certificate that represents shares bought at different times or different prices. In that case, assuming you're using a broker to sell the shares, you need to identify the shares you're selling (as explained below) when you deliver the certificate to the broker. If you sell some of the stock represented by a certificate *without* using a broker or other agent, you simply have to maintain a written record of which shares you sold.

How to Identify Shares

Now we come to the meat of the question. You left your shares with your broker and you want to sell some but not all of them. To identify the shares you're selling you need to do two things:

- *At the time of the sale,* specify to the broker the shares you're selling, *and*

- *Within a reasonable time thereafter,* receive a written confirmation of that specification from your broker.

Clearing the Air

Before we go another step let's clear up the biggest point of confusion. The traditional way to specify the shares you're selling is in the form of an instruction to your broker:

Sell 50 shares XYZ from the lot purchased on March 12, 1998.

This makes it sound like the broker has to do something special—possibly locate those specific shares, or at least make a record of some kind indicating what shares you sold. Some brokers say, "We don't offer that service." But in reality the only thing the broker has to do, besides executing the sale transaction in the normal way, is send you a written confirmation that you specified shares from the lot purchased on March 12, 1998.

Only part of the message shown above is really an instruction. "Sell 50 shares XYZ" is an instruction. The rest of the message is there for the sole purpose of establishing proof acceptable to the IRS that you made a choice at the time of the sale. *Your broker doesn't have to do anything about the second part of the message—except provide written confirmation that they received it.*

If I seem to be shouting here, it's because I've seen brokers time and again misunderstand this rule. They'll tell you it's okay to do your own identification on your tax return, or that their computers aren't set up to handle this, or some other nonsense. Tell them that's all very nice but you need written confirmation of your identification.

Specifying the Shares

When you specify the shares to be sold, you need to identify the shares in a way that makes it clear which shares you sold. Any of the following might do the trick:

- The shares I bought on March 12, 1998.

- The shares I bought for 40-3/8.

- The shares I bought most recently.

In theory, it shouldn't matter if the instruction is meaningless to the broker. For example, you may have had a different broker when you bought the shares, so the present broker has no idea what shares you bought on March 12, 1998. The thing that *does* matter is that your choice is objective and unambiguous, so you can prove to the IRS which shares you sold.

If you do your trading online, you may find that there's no apparent way to give instructions as to which shares you're selling. If you're in this situation, it should be acceptable if you send an email at the same time as your order, saying something like this:

My sale order # 123456 pertains to shares pur-chased on March 12, 1998. Please acknowledge in writing that you received this message at the time of the sale.

I don't guaranty that they'll respond in writing, but in my view this procedure will work if you can get them to do so. The regulations say you have to specify the shares at the time of the sale, but they don't require you to specify them as part of the process of giving the sale order.

> ▪ Be careful not to send an email that can be misinterpreted as an *additional* sale order.

Instruction need not be in writing. Although you need confirmation from the broker in writing, your *instruction* does *not* have to be in writing. It can be given by email, or orally over the telephone.

Broker's Confirmation

The second requirement is that you receive written confirmation of the identification from the broker within a reasonable time after the transaction. Remember, they're merely confirming *your message*. They don't have to confirm that they actually sold those specific shares. *All you need is written confirmation that you identified the stock at the time of the sale.*

Example: Your broker sends you a message stating "We acknowledge that you identified the 500 shares of XYZ sold on May 18, 2004 as shares purchased on March 12, 1998."

That's it! If you can extract that in writing from your broker within a reasonable time after the sale, you've met the requirement. Traditional brokers who know how to handle identification may acknowledge the identification on the trade confirmation slip, but this isn't a requirement. You just need something in writing that confirms your identification.

Email? No one knows for sure whether email confirmation is good enough because there's no guidance on this question. The regulations require a *written document* from your broker, and it's possible the IRS will say that email doesn't pass muster. You're safer if you can get your broker to send confirmation of your instructions by regular mail.

> **Note:** One taxpayer won a case where all of the communications were oral, and there was no written confirmation from his broker. I think the result of that case is questionable, so I'm reluctant to rely on it.

Blanket Instructions

Some advisors suggest that you can give your broker a blanket instruction, such as "always sell the shares with the highest basis." If you have written confirmation of such an instruction from your broker it should stand up in court. Bear in mind, though, that there may be times when you want to use a different approach. For example, it may be better to sell the shares with a lower basis because they produce long-term capital gain instead of short-term gain. You may get better results if you make a specific identification each time you sell some but not all of your shares.

Separate Accounts

The regulations don't mention the possibility of holding your shares in separate accounts. It's reasonably clear, though, that if you do so, the separate accounts serve as at least a partial identification of the shares you're selling. If you sell the shares in Account A, you don't have to specify that you aren't selling the shares in Account B, because that's already clear. It may make sense to keep your ISO shares in a separate account from any other shares you own, for example.

Chapter 51
The Wash Sale Rule

People who trade stocks often run into the wash sale rule, and you may encounter it in connection with stock you receive from your company, too. This rule prevents you from claiming a loss from a sale of stock if you buy replacement stock in the same company shortly before or after the sale.

> ▪ The wash sale rule applies only to losses. You can't use the wash sale rule to avoid reporting a gain by purchasing replacement stock.

General Rule

In general you have a wash sale if you sell stock at a loss, and buy substantially identical securities within 30 days before or after the sale.

> **Example:** On March 31 you sell 100 shares of XYZ at a loss. On April 10 you buy 100 shares of XYZ. The sale on March 31 is a wash sale.

The *wash sale period* for any sale at a loss consists of 61 days: the day of the sale, the 30 days before the sale and the 30 days after the sale. (These are calendar days, not trading days. Count carefully!) For a sale on March 31, the wash sale period includes all of March and April. If you want to claim your loss as a deduction, you need to avoid purchasing the same stock during the wash sale period.

Consequences of a Wash Sale

The wash sale will actually have *three* consequences:

- You aren't allowed to claim the loss on your sale.

- Your disallowed loss is added to the basis of the replacement stock.

- Your holding period for the replacement stock includes the holding period of the stock you sold.

The first one is clear enough, but the others may require some explanation.

Basis Adjustment

The basis adjustment is important: it preserves the benefit of the disallowed loss. You'll receive that benefit on a future sale of the replacement stock.

> **Example:** Some time ago you bought 80 shares of XYZ at $50. The stock has declined to $30, and you sell it to take the loss deduction. But then you see some good news on XYZ and buy it back for $32, less than 31 days after the sale
>
> You can't deduct your loss of $20 per share. But you add $20 per share to the basis of your replacement shares. Those shares have a basis of $52 per share: the $32 you paid, plus the $20 wash sale adjustment. In other words, you're treated as if you bought the shares for $52. If you end up selling them for $55, you'll only report $3 per share of gain. If you sell them for $32 (the same price you paid to buy them), you'll report a loss of $20 per share.

Because of this basis adjustment, a wash sale usually isn't a disaster. In most cases, it simply means you'll get the same tax benefit at a later time. If you receive the benefit later in the same year, the wash sale may have no effect at all on your taxes.

There are times, though, when the wash sale rule can have truly painful consequences:

- If you don't sell the replacement stock in the same year, your loss will be postponed, possibly to a year when the deduction is of far less value.

- If you die before selling the replacement stock, neither you nor your heirs will benefit from the basis adjustment.

- You can also lose the benefit of the deduction permanently if you try to get around the wash sale rule by using your IRA to buy replacement stock. There's no clear guidance on this issue, but I believe the IRS can disallow the loss permanently in this situation.

Holding Period

When you make a wash sale, your holding period for the replacement stock includes the period you held the stock you sold. This rule prevents you from converting a long-term loss into a short-term loss.

Example: You've held shares of XYZ for years and it's been a dog. You sell it at a loss but then buy it back within the wash sale period. When you sell the replacement stock, your gain or loss will be long-term—no matter how soon you sell it.

In some situations you get more tax savings from a short-term loss than a long-term loss, so this rule generally works against you.

Chapter 52
Protecting Gains Without Selling

When your stock or options become very valuable, it makes sense to think about protecting your gains. The simplest way to do this may be to exercise the options and sell the stock. The tax consequences of that action may be painful, though. Are there ways you can protect your gains without incurring the tax consequences?

The answer is a qualified yes. There are some things you can do, but you run into some complicated rules that are explained in more detail in my book, *Capital Gains, Minimal Taxes*. This chapter lays out some of the main points.

Short Sales

One way to protect a built-in gain is through a *short sale*. When you sell short, some or all of the loss you have from a decline in the value of your stock or options will cancel out. This technique provides limited tax benefits, however:

- A short sale is treated as a disqualifying disposition of immature ISO stock or ESPP stock.

- A short sale prevents your stock from "aging" for purposes of getting long-term capital gain when you sell it.

- A short sale may be treated as a *constructive sale* in the year of the short sale, rather than in a later year when you dispose of your stock.

How a short sale works. A short sale is a transaction in which you sell stock that's owned by someone else. If you tell your broker to sell 100 shares of XYZ short, your broker will *borrow* 100 shares from another account and sell them. Your account gets credit for the cash, and you owe a debt: not a cash debt, but an obligation to pay back the stock you borrowed. In stock market lingo, you now have a *short position* in the stock.

A regular stock owner—someone with a *long* position—is hoping that the price of the stock will go up. When you're short, the opposite is true. If the price of the stock goes up, you'll have to pay more to buy the shares you need to repay your debt. You'll make money if the stock goes down, because then you can buy the stock cheaply and return the shares you sold earlier when the price was higher.

> **Example:** When the price of XYZ is $35 you sell 100 shares short. Your brokerage account gets credit for $3,500. Later, you satisfy your obligation to return the 100 shares of XYZ by buying them at $32. You're left with a profit of $300, less brokerage commissions.

> ▪ When you have a short position, you're in exactly the opposite stance from someone who owns the stock. You make money when the stock goes down, and lose when it goes up.

Usual tax treatment. Generally speaking, you don't report any income or gain at the time you make a short sale. Even though you received money when you made the short sale, you don't know yet whether you're going to have a gain or loss. You find that out when you close the short sale by delivering the stock you owe. The cost of the stock you use to close the short sale determines whether you have a gain or a loss on the transaction. Limitations on this tax treatment are discussed below.

Short against the box. The strange thing about selling short is that you can do it even if you already own shares in that company. For example, if you own 100 shares of XYZ and want to sell 100, you can either sell the shares you own—or keep the shares you own and make a short sale. On Wall Street they call this going *short against the box.*

If you're short against the box, you've neutralized your market position. If the stock price goes up, the value of the shares you hold will increase, but the value of your short position will go down by the same amount. A similar cancellation occurs if the stock price goes down.

Selling short against the box would seem to be an ideal way to lock in your gains without paying tax:

> **Example:** You have 1,000 shares of your company's stock from exercising a nonqualified option. The stock price has gone sky high since you exercised the option. If you sell the stock, you'll have to report a large gain. Worse, the gain will be short term because you exercised the option less than a year ago. You're worried that the stock price may be ready to dive.
>
> Instead of selling the stock you own, you instruct your broker to make a short sale against the box. Because you've sold borrowed stock, instead of stock you own, you don't report gain or loss on the short sale. You have the cash from the sale, though, so you've locked in your gains from the stock. Later, you'll have a choice: you can close the short sale using the shares you already own, or buy new shares to close the short sale.

Unfortunately, as explained next, the tax law stands in the way of this elegant solution to your problem.

Limitations on Using Short Sales

In an ideal world you would be able to use a short sale in this manner to protect the gain in your stock or options indefinitely while avoiding negative tax consequences. The tax law isn't that generous, however. Here are the main limitations on using this approach:

Immature ISO and ESPP stock. A short sale against the box should not be used to protect gains in stock from an incentive stock option or employee stock purchase plan before you've satisfied the special holding period. The IRS says this is a disqualifying disposition of the stock. That means you have to report compensation income at the time you make the short sale, even if you eventually use other stock to close the short sale.

Short-term holding period. If your stock has a short-term holding period when you make the short sale, its holding period will re-start when you close the short sale. As a result, the short sale may prevent you from using long-term capital gain rates when you eventually sell your stock.

> **Example:** You've held your stock for nine months, and the price has gone up substantially in that period of time. To protect your gain, you make a short sale against the box. Six months later you buy stock in the open market to close the short sale. You still own the original stock, and you've held it more than a year. Nevertheless, any gain from this stock will be short-term unless you hold it at least a year and a day beyond the date you closed the short sale.

This rule doesn't apply if the stock was already long-term at the time you entered into the short sale. In the example above, if you held the stock at least a year and a day before you made the short sale, any gain or loss on sale of the stock would be long-term. There's a rub, here, though. If you have a loss on the short sale, you'll have to treat that as a long-term loss. That may reduce the benefit of receiving a long-term gain from this stock or from other transactions.

Constructive sales. It gets worse. At one time it was possible to be short against the box for an indefinite period of time without having to report income or gain. The law now provides that you have to report a *constructive sale* of your stock if you're short against the box for an extended period of time. The rule applies only to *appreciated financial positions*—in other words, stock or options that would produce a gain if you sold them for fair market value.

To avoid a constructive sale, you need to close the short position by January 30 of the year after you established it, and continue to hold the long position (the stock) without a protective short position for at least 60 days. Otherwise you'll be treated as if you sold the original stock on the day you entered into the short sale.

> **Example:** You hold stock that has gone up in value since you bought it. In November, you make a short sale against the box. If you continue to hold the short position at the end of the following January, you'll have to report a sale of the stock in the year you made the short sale.
>
> To avoid this, you buy stock on the open market on January 20 and use this stock to close your short position. You continue to own the original shares. You'll still have to report a sale in the previous year if you establish a new short position in the following 60 days. If you bear the market risk of holding the stock *without* an offsetting short position for at least 60 days, you avoid having to report gain in the year of your short sale.

Using Market Options

Another possible way to protect your profits without selling your stock is to use *market options*—options you buy and sell through a broker. You can hedge against the risk of loss on your stock by buying a put option, or selling a call option—or both.

A *call option* is the same type of option you receive from your employer. It provides the holder with the right to purchase stock at a specified price. A *put option* provides the holder with the right to *sell* the stock at a specified price.

> **Example:** You hold 1,000 shares of your company's stock, and they have gone up in value since you

acquired them. You buy 10 put options (each put option applies to 100 shares) to sell at the current price. If the stock's price plummets, you can exercise the put option, forcing the person who sold the option to buy the stock at the favorable price that prevailed at the time you bought the option.

If the price goes up or stays the same, you won't exercise the put option. You'll lose the cost of the put option, but you won't complain because it acted as an insurance policy against the stock going down.

Selling a call option provides protection in a different way. You don't gain direct protection against the stock going down in value because you don't have a right to force a sale. But you've received a payment for the option (called the option *premium*), and that payment will at least partially offset any loss you have from a decline in the value of the stock. When you sell a call option, you give up the benefit of a future increase in the value of your stock, because the option will be exercised if the stock price goes up.

In some situations, people do *both*. They buy a put option and sell a call option at the same time. It may be possible to select options that have matching prices: the cost of the put option is the same as the amount you receive for selling the call option. In stock market lingo, this is a *costless collar*. It didn't cost you anything to put it in place, and it puts an upper and lower limit on your profit from the stock.

Unfortunately, these techniques invoke many complicated rules, and some of the issues don't have clear answers. The rules are so technical that you may have a hard time finding a tax professional who is well versed in them. What follows is the tip of the iceberg:

Immature ISO and ESPP stock. You shouldn't be considered to have made a disqualifying disposition of your immature stock from an incentive stock option or employee stock purchase plan if you buy a put option or sell a call option, provided that the option isn't in the money at the time you do this. The contrary may be true if the option is in the money, or if you do *both* (buy a put and sell a call).

Short-term holding period. Here again you can end up with a short-term holding period even after you've held the stock more than a year. This is part of a very complicated set of rules called the *straddle rules,* and works much like the short sale rule described above.

Constructive sales. You can have a constructive sale as a result of option transactions, just as you can from a short sale against the box. You shouldn't have a constructive sale if you buy a put or sell a call when the option isn't in the money. If the option is in the money, or you use both techniques at once, you may have a constructive sale.

Loss deferral. If the combination of your stock holdings and your option position is a *straddle* under the tax rules, you can't claim a loss from one position if you have an unrecognized gain in the other position.

The straddle rules are quite complicated. They include rules under which you can avoid some of the negative consequences of holding a straddle if you sell *qualified covered calls.* Details on these rules are beyond the scope of this book.

Chapter 53
Reporting Sales of Stock

When you sell stock through a broker you'll receive a form reporting the results of that sale: Form 1099-B. This form does *not* tell how much gain or loss to report. It merely tells how much you received from the sale. It's up to you to figure how much gain or loss you report from the sale, and whether the gain or loss is long-term or short-term. If you don't report your full basis in the stock, you may inadvertently pay tax on the same income twice.

Chapters describing different types of transactions (such as exercise of nonqualified options or incentive stock options) tell how to determine your *basis* and your *holding period.* You need those two pieces of information, in addition to the amount of *proceeds* from the sale, to report the sale on your return. Generally, sale proceeds are equal to the sale price of the stock minus any brokerage commissions, SEC fee and other selling expenses.

> • The SEC fee is a small fraction of the selling price for shares sold in the stock markets, which is used to fund enforcement efforts of the SEC. Unless you sell a huge amount of stock, this fee will be tiny.

Schedule D

You report capital gains and losses on Schedule D, which is an attachment to Form 1040. The front of that form is in two parts, one for short-term gain or loss and one for long-term gain or loss. So the first thing you need to know is whether your holding period is a year or less (short-term) or at least a year and a day (long-term). If you sell exactly on the first anniversary of the day you acquired the stock, your gain or loss is short-term. Once you have the right part of the form, proceed as follows:

- In column (a) write a simple description of what you sold. There's an example right on the form: "100 sh XYZ Co."

- In column (b) write the date acquired. Use the date that measures your holding period, rather than the date you literally acquired the stock. For example, if the stock wasn't vested when you received it, and you didn't make the section 83b election, use the date the stock *vested* as the date acquired. If you made a single sale of shares that were acquired on more than one date, write "various" in this column. But don't combine long-term and short-term shares in a single group, even if you sold them all at once.

- In column (c) write the date of sale. For stock sold on a stock exchange, this is the *trade date*, not the settlement date.

- Column (d) on the form is labeled "sales price." If you received a Form 1099-B for the sale (as you should have if you sold your stock through a broker) you should report the same number here as appears on the Form 1099-B. Otherwise, report the proceeds from the sale minus any selling expenses.

- Column (e) is where you report your cost or other basis. Be sure to include any amount reported as compensation when you acquired the stock (or when it vested). Also, if your broker didn't subtract the brokerage commission and other selling expenses when reporting your sale proceeds on Form 1099-B, you have to add those items to your basis.

- Subtract the number in column (e) from the number in column (d), and write the result in column (f). If the number is positive, you have a capital gain. If the number is negative, indicate this by writing it in parentheses. Some software programs use a minus sign instead of parentheses and that's okay too, but easier to miss when reading a return quickly.

Follow the rest of the instructions for this form to combine your gain or loss with any other capital gains and losses, then transfer the number to the appropriate line on Form 1040.

> ▪ **Long-term gain? Caution:** Many people forget that they need to do a special rate calculation if they have a long-term capital gain. This is where you get your tax savings from the special capital gains rate, so don't make this mistake! If you're preparing the return yourself without the aid of tax software, you'll have to follow instructions carefully. It's worth the effort, because it lowers your taxes.

The IRS wants you to attach an explanation if you use something other than the actual cost of the stock as your basis. You might attach a statement that looks something like this:

John Q. Public

SSN 123-45-6789

2002 Form 1040, Schedule D

The basis used for 1000 shares of XYZ stock includes $25,000 of compensation income reported in 2001 in connection with the purchase of the shares pursuant to a nonqualified stock option.

Resources

Taxation of Stock Transactions

Capital Gains, Minimal Taxes: The Essential Guide for Investors and Traders by Kaye A. Thomas (Fairmark Press Inc. 2001). A plain language explanation of all tax rules, from the most basic to the most advanced, that apply to people who buy and sell stocks, mutual funds and stock options. For details and ordering information:

www.fairmark.com/books/cgmt.htm

Web Site for Option Advisors

National Board of Certified Option Advisors (on the web at www.nbcoa.com). This organization provides training materials and a certification exam for tax professionals and financial advisors who help option holders handle stock options and other forms of equity compensation.

Web Sites for Option Holders

Fairmark Press Tax Guide for Investors (web site at www.fairmark.com). This site offers more information on many of the topics covered in this book. You'll find a section where we post updates, corrections and clarifications to this book, and a message board where you can post comments and ask questions.

National Board of Certified Option Advisors (on the web at www.nbcoa.com). This web site offers information for option holders as well as option advisors, including how to select someone to help plan your stock option strategy.

myStockOptions.com. This web site has a wealth of materials dealing with stock options and related subjects.

Other Books for Option Holders

In this growing field, the following books are among the most helpful:

Stock Options: Getting Your Share of the Action, by Tom Taulli (Bloomberg Press 2001)

Your Employee Stock Options, by Alan B. Ungar and Mark T. Sakanashi (Harper Business, 2001)

Stock Options: An Authoritative Guide to Incentive and Nonqualified Stock Options, by Robert R. Pastore (PCM Capital Publishing 1999)

The Employee's Guide to Stock Options, by Corey Rosen (The National Center for Employee Ownership 2002)—*not to be confused with:*

An Employee's Guide to Stock Options, by Beth V. Walker (McGraw-Hill 2003)

Web Sites for Companies and Administrators

Certified Equity Professional Institute (cepi.scu.edu). This unit of Santa Clara University provides training and a certification exam for people who manage or administer stock option plans for companies.

National Center for Employee Ownership (www.nceo.org). A membership organization that focuses on ways to provide equity ownership to employees. NCEO publishes some of the leading books on stock options and holds meetings and seminars.

Foundation for Enterprise Development (www.fed.org). FED also publishes materials and holds seminars on employee ownership.

National Association of Stock Plan Professionals (www.naspp.com). Membership organization for those involved in administering stock plans.

Index

also from Fairmark Press:

Capital Gains, Minimal Taxes
The Essential Guide for Investors and Traders

This book makes it easy to understand the rules—and the best strategies for minimizing taxes. In plain language it covers:

- **Buying and selling stocks.** Complete coverage of relevant tax provisions, including the capital loss limitation, how to identify shares and the wash sale rule.

- **Mutual fund investments.** How and when to use the averaging rules for sales of mutual fund shares, and a guide to all the categories of mutual fund dividends.

- **Rules for advanced investors.** Clear explanation of tax rules for short sales, stock options and "straddles."

- **Tax treatment of traders.** Find out if your buying and selling activity qualifies you as a trader—and if so, how that will affect your taxes.

Capital Gains, Minimal Taxes is your complete, authoritative guide to taxation of stocks, mutual funds and market-traded stock options.

Capital Gains, Minimal Taxes:
The Essential Guide for Investors and Traders
by Kaye A. Thomas
Fairmark Press Inc.
ISBN 0967498147
306 pages
$23.95

Order Form

Order more copies of either of our books from our web site (**www.fairmark.com**), or by mailing or faxing a copy of this form.

Fax: (630) 434-0753   Mail: Fairmark Press Inc.
                                                    P.O. Box 353
                                                    Lisle, IL 60532

Quantity

_____   *Consider Your Options* @ $23.95   _____

_____   *Capital Gains, Minimal Taxes* @ $23.95   _____

                          Total for books   _____

          Shipping (flat rate per order)   _____ $4.00

          Total   _____

Illinois residents add $1.62 per book sales tax.

Ship to:

Name: _____

Address: _____

Address: _____

City, State, zip: _____

Phone: _____

Email: _____

Payment

____ Check   ____ VISA   ____ MasterCard
                          ____ AMEX   ____ Discover

Card number: _____

Exp. date: _____

Credit Card Info (if different from shipping)

Billing name: _____

Address: _____

City, State, zip: _____